Puppet ministry made easy

Dale & Liz VonSeggen

Loveland, Colorado

Group's R.E.A.L. Guarantee to you:

This Group resource incorporates our R.E.A.L. approach to ministry—one that encourages long-term retention and life transformation. It's ministry that's:

Relational
Because learner-to-learner interaction enhances learning and builds Christian friendships.

Experiential
Because what learners experience through discussion and action sticks with them up to 9 times longer than what they simply hear or read.

Applicable
Because the aim of Christian education is to equip learners to be both hearers and doers of God's Word.

Learner-based
Because learners understand and retain more when the learning process takes into consideration how they learn best.

Puppet Ministry Made Easy
Copyright © 1990 and 2003 by Dale and Liz VonSeggen
2003 edition

Visit our Web site: **www.grouppublishing.com**

• •

Credits
Editors: Amy Nappa and Karl Leuthauser
Chief Creative Officer: Joani Schultz
Copy Editor: Linda Marcinkowski
Art Director: Randy Kady
Print Production Artist: Joyce Douglas
Illustrator: Matt Wood
Cover Art Director/Designer: Bambi Eitel
Cover Photographer: Daniel Treat
Production Manager: DeAnne Lear

Custom Puppets supplied for cover by: One Way Street, Inc., P.O. Box 5077, Englewood, CO 80155-5077; 303-790-1188; **www.onewaystreet.com**

Library of Congress Cataloging-in-Publication Data
VonSeggen, Dale.
Puppet ministry made easy / by Dale and Liz VonSeggen.
   p. cm.
ISBN 0-7644-2525-0 (pbk. : alk. paper)
1. Puppet theater in Christian education. I. VonSeggen, Liz. II. Title.
BV1535.9.P8 V66 2002
246'.725--dc21
   2002013818

10 9 8 7 6 5 4 3 2 1   12 11 10 09 08 07 06 05 04 03
Printed in the United States of America.

Dedication

We dedicate this book to all our staff at One Way Street who have been our co-workers in reaching and teaching thousands of young people and their leaders about successful puppet ministry. Thanks for your faithfulness even when nobody noticed your individual contributions. God did notice and He has blessed your efforts across the years and around the world!

Contents

Introduction

Puppets have caught the attention of audiences down through history, helping people laugh, pretend, dream, empathize, and learn new ideas. In the past thirty years, puppets have invaded the church. Groups of teenagers, families, teachers, missionaries, and others around the world are discovering an effective "work of their hands" through puppet ministry.

But just what is puppet ministry? It can be different things to different people. It can be a segment of a ministry, where several puppeteers and a director use puppets to reach out to children, the handicapped, those in nursing homes, or youth groups.

Some groups use puppets in inner-city ministries and on mission trips to Indian reservations. Others sponsor neighborhood "backyard Bible clubs" in the summer to reach children who may otherwise never hear of Jesus.

Choirs and singing groups often use puppets to add variety, drama, and excitement to choir tours and performances.

Several puppet teams have each remodeled a church bus and installed carpeting, a sound system, and a puppet stage (in the back end of the bus). Then they've used the brightly painted, attention-getting vehicle as a mobile puppet theater. They drive the "puppet bus" into parks and neighborhoods to entertain and inspire children and adults.

Countless churches, groups, and individuals in the United States and around the world have discovered that a colorful handful of foam rubber, fake fur, and cloth can become a ministry tool with eternal results. And puppet ministry provides a fun opportunity for volunteers to share their faith and to learn how to work together as a team.

When children's pastor Norm Hewitt arrived at his new position in a Florida church, he found the remnants of a dead puppet team. Several older children and young teens had been involved, but the team had fizzled out. They never had regular practices or performances and because of low morale and a lack of leadership, most of the kids had dropped out.

Norm teamed up with one of the parents and in just a few weeks presented a Christmas puppet special for the entire church. Although it was only one puppet song performed as an offertory, it resulted in much excitement and desire to form a "new" puppet team. With a fresh vision of what puppet ministry could become, several kids expressed interest and joined the puppet team. They not only became skilled in puppetry but grew in their relationship with God and in leadership. Out of this team came many leaders of the youth group, as their puppet ministry experience helped make a real difference in their lives.

Kids who have been actively involved in puppet ministry have expressed their delight in the joy an audience experiences. One sixth-grader said it this way, "It's really fun to hear the audience laugh and clap, and to know God is using me to tell everyone about his love."

So what about you and your church? Why not join the thousands who have discovered the impact puppet ministry can have, both on the lives of audiences and on the spiritual growth of puppet team members.

How to Use This Book

This book takes you step by step through establishing a puppet ministry in your church. The guidelines and tips in these pages will help you

- ♦ develop a vision for puppet ministry in your church;
- ♦ recruit kids and adults to commit to puppet ministry;
- ♦ involve others in directing the ministry;
- ♦ choose your puppets;
- ♦ choose scripts;
- ♦ write scripts;
- ♦ build a puppet stage;

* plan effective rehearsals; and
* put together a complete program.

We'll even give you instructions for taking your puppet team on the road—touching lives by presenting programs to a variety of audiences.

Whether you have volunteers beating down your door for a chance to work with puppets or you're starting out solo, this book provides the tools you need to take puppetry into your church and community. Take an afternoon or two and thoroughly read the entire book. Treat it as a workbook. Highlight critical points. Scribble notes and comments in the margins. Bend it. Stuff it in your pocket or purse. It's OK. It's here to serve you.

But whatever you do, don't leave it lying on the shelf! Let the book act as your guide through the many decisions you must make.

Puppetry has been a lasting source of joy and challenge for us in the many years we've worked in it. The lighthearted message of love conveyed by puppets rarely fails in getting people to open up and look at their hearts. And often it leads them to the one who can meet their every need: Jesus.

That's what makes puppets and puppetry fun and meaningful. So enjoy! Catch the puppet ministry vision and share it with those around you. Before long you'll find yourself sharing God's love through your hands.

CHAPTER 1

Why Puppet Ministry?

About twenty years ago, a Chicago area housewife named Christy Watkins attended a Christian education conference in a Chicago suburb. She had been very active in children's ministry in her church, directing children's choirs and using drama with the choir musicals. She was attracted to a certain classroom by the noise of a large crowd and went in to discover a puppet ministry workshop in progress. To put it mildly, Christy was stricken with a severe case of "puppet fever." Her life, and the life of her church, would never be the same again.

Some time later, she went to watch a touring puppet team perform a complete children's musical with puppets, and the wheels of her very creative mind started turning.

Christy, with the dedicated assistance of her husband Jerry, her four children, and two other faithful church families, recruited many more puppeteers to form a ministry called the P.O.W.E.R. Company, which stands for "Puppet Outreach Working for Eternal Results."

Christy and her team have been ministering with puppets, drama, music, signing, and mime since 1980. They have performed all across the United States, Canada, and Mexico and have been featured numerous times at regional and national puppet ministry and children's ministry conferences.

Christy reflects over her past twenty-two years of puppet ministry leadership experience: "Puppet ministry has been a way to share my faith while doing what I love to do, which is being involved in the lives of young people. It has been a unique combination of ministry and being ministered to. Through the last twenty-two years of puppetry, my husband and I have seen our own four children, and over 150 other children and teens who have been through the program, experience success, have a heart for ministry, and draw closer to God. It has been an opportunity to develop my creativity and to challenge me to dig deeper in my own faith. We thank God for giving us this ministry. It has been a privilege and blessing for our whole family."

Benefits of Puppet Ministry

When someone views a puppet presentation, he or she sees only the end result of hours spent building stages and props and rehearsing. Since puppetry is lighthearted and fun, people often fail to realize not only the work that goes into it but also the long-lasting—even eternal—results it can have in people's lives.

An active puppet ministry can provide a means to disciple others who are interested in performing and developing a ministry in the church and community. Unlike drama or choir, puppetry allows shy, non-verbal, or non-musical people to excel in a performance field and find an effective way to minister. Of course, outgoing volunteers will also enjoy the unique fun of puppetry and the ministry it can offer.

A well-rounded, effective puppet ministry focuses on three areas: the group, the church, and the community.

Ministry in the group—Since puppet ministry is generally a small-group effort, make the puppet team and its rehearsals a place where team members can share prayer requests and personal concerns, and learn to care for others.

Many teams spend fifteen to thirty minutes at the beginning of every rehearsal for Bible study or sharing time. Other groups establish prayer partners within the team. Often team members go to fun events together—just as friends. Without this openness and personal concern for one another within the team, outside ministries will be less effective.

As team members rehearse, build props, travel together, pray, and share experiences in a small-group setting, many positive things happen. Ministry members gain self-confidence, learn to reach out to new people, and grow in their understanding of themselves and God.

Ministry in the church—Often, puppet ministry in the local church is put into a box labeled "For Children Only," and many exciting avenues for ministry close off. Puppets work well as tools to minister to, teach, and entertain all ages. You only need to choose skits and songs appropriate to the audience you want to reach. Use puppet ministry in your children's church, Sunday school classes, adult banquets and parties, youth group meetings, worship services, after-church gatherings, and senior adult activities.

Ministry to the community—The puppet team is a "natural" when it comes to making an impact outside the walls of the church.

Active puppet ministries often find open doors to minister in places other ministry forms find difficult. For example, puppets are usually welcomed into public schools and many civic clubs or organizations—places evangelists or even Christian drama groups might find hard to penetrate. The fantasy aspect of puppetry makes it seem less "threatening" than other forms of Christian outreach. And the results—in terms of puppeteers' lives and the lives of those they touch—are immeasurable.

A Philosophy of Puppet Ministry

Puppets are wonderful fantasy characters who can take audiences on enchanting trips into the imagination. Fun is their foundation and exaggeration is their primary tool. But behind all the curtains and props, successful puppetry relies on several basic principles. Let's look at these.

Puppets are fantasy characters. They don't have a heart or a soul. They can be compared to cartoon characters such as Scooby-Doo or Arthur. They aren't real.

For this reason, puppets never "get saved." However, a puppet may sometimes take on the role of a character who's a Christian or even act out a scene in which a character becomes a Christian. But the puppet itself should never ask Jesus into its heart—it doesn't have one!

Here's an example to help clarify this issue. Let's say you have a puppet you generally call Roscoe. Now since Roscoe is a puppet, he should never pray for salvation or go through any kind of conversion experience. However, in a particular skit, Roscoe may play the part of the Apostle Paul on the road to Damascus. In that case, Roscoe would act out Paul's conversion—but only as a puppet imitating a real person.

Puppets don't model negative behavior as acceptable. This includes name-calling, hitting, or using bad language. Of course, a puppet may act the part of an evil character who puts down Christianity and challenges the truth. But it should be obvious that the character's attitudes and behavior are wrong.

Puppets don't misuse humor. Puppets usually find success whenever they use humor, but a performance must never make light of spiritual truths. A sprinkling of good humor is usually more effective than a constant barrage of jokes strung through a presentation.

A presentation may start with light material or use a light piece somewhere in the middle for comic relief. But it must end with a serious point. Closing songs and skits should have a thoughtful impact on the audience—not leave them laughing hysterically. Compromising your message for humor diminishes your ministry's effectiveness.

◆   ◆   ◆   ◆   ◆

These principles can help you when planning presentations. Good puppetry is good theater. Keep your purpose in mind as you prepare, then work creatively to build God's kingdom in your church and community through puppets.

CHAPTER 2

Getting Started

The introduction of this book talks about Norm Hewitt and his part in resurrecting the puppet team at his church. Well, Norm knew that by setting a regular rehearsal schedule, choosing songs and skits he knew his puppeteers would like, and investing himself personally in the lives of his team members, he could get some excitement going.

But he also knew that this excitement would fade if the team didn't perform regularly. He made sure they had several performances scheduled, and then he used an upcoming regional puppetry festival and competition to give his team an opportunity to travel and share its ministry outside the church. After three months of local church rehearsals and performances, his team competed at the festival and won a gold medal!

Before long Norm had more kids wanting to join the team than he could handle. The team grew in size and in impact in the local area. With twenty-four puppeteers and six adult directors, they began to minister at local fairs, day-care centers, churches, and public schools. Several team members took part in a mission trip to Nicaragua, where over twelve hundred children heard about Jesus through the puppets.

Norm experienced success because he did a lot of things right, covering everything with enthusiasm and prayer. Let's take a look at some of the factors to consider as you begin your puppet team ministry.

The Team Size

Your puppet team may have any number of members, but a team with five to eight members and one or two adult directors usually works best. If your church has several adults to help lead, you might choose to have twelve to fifteen members. But keep the team small at first so you can work more effectively with each puppeteer. Then increase numbers as performance skills and commitment increase.

How do you get potential puppeteers through the door? You can spark interest in several ways. For example, invite a quality puppet team to perform. Take your potential team to see a puppet team rehearse. Or better yet, attend a puppet ministry training seminar.

Evaluate your church's situation to determine how you'll recruit your team. Some leaders hold auditions. But one-on-one recruiting often works best. Some leaders also talk to all their kids and parents together, then build their team with those who'll commit to an ongoing puppet team ministry.

The Team Members

How should a puppet team be put together? Who should be involved? It all depends on your focus and your purposes. Puppet teams come in all shapes and sizes—some with just two kids the same age, some with thirty kids ranging from ages ten to eighteen, others comprised entirely of adults. However, certain membership combinations work better than others.

For example, puppet teams usually work best when the members are about the same age. This makes it easier to select the size of puppets and height of the stage so everyone can participate. A team with members from fourth grade through high school might work, but two different teams with similarly-aged puppeteers may work better. Many puppet ministries find a team of fifth- and sixth-graders to be especially valuable as it provides special identity and ministry opportunity for the preteens.

Anyone can become an excellent puppeteer, but certain people are particularly drawn to this ministry. Do you have any shy children or adults in your church? They are perfect puppeteer prospects. Since all performing happens behind a curtain, puppetry gives quiet volunteers a great creative outlet. Puppetry also builds their self-confidence.

Other potential puppeteers are those who like music but really don't like to—or can't—sing. Puppetry may be just the place for these church members to get involved. They can perform without singing themselves. Drama buffs or "hams" are other good prospects. Puppetry is a natural outlet for these performers.

Perhaps your group includes a "loner." Since puppet teams are generally small, tightknit groups, they can become exactly what that loner needs to form friendships.

Probably the most important advice for the beginning puppet director is: Get help! Recruit assistance for the many jobs involved in puppet ministry. Adults or kids with sound equipment experience, artistic ability, sewing expertise, organizational skills, and even counseling ability will be invaluable to the ministry. Many volunteers have hidden talents a puppet ministry could utilize. And giving team members responsibility will give them a greater sense of ownership in the ministry.

Volunteers can fill many roles in your puppet team ministry:

- Running the sound system
- Running the light system
- Cleaning and helping organize the puppet storage area
- Labeling puppet boxes and prop areas
- Acting as puppet caretakers who change costumes and comb the puppets' hair for performances
- Acting as prop caretakers who repair any broken props and make sure they are stored carefully
- Assisting with prop making
- Phoning team members to remind them of rehearsal and performance details
- Leading devotions or sharing prayer requests
- Setting up the stage and putting it away
- Giving creative input for puppet skits and songs
- Assisting newcomers with basic skills
- Taking turns planning the choreography for a puppet song
- Bringing refreshments for puppet rehearsal

As the team director, recruit enough leaders that if you were removed from the picture, the ministry would continue. Too often a puppet team's leadership focuses on one individual. And if that individual moves away, loses interest, or becomes discouraged, the ministry dies.

The Defined Ministry

When Don began a puppet ministry team some years ago, many group members were skeptical. They weren't convinced that using puppets was an effective way to minister. But the puppet team has grown into a powerful ministry.

Among other accomplishments, Don's team has

* taken two summer ministry tours;
* performed several full-length musicals;
* performed in area public schools; and
* hosted a training festival for kids from area churches.

But Don's team hasn't done everything. For example, Don's team has never

* performed in a nursing home;
* performed in a prison or a juvenile home;
* worked with kids in children's hospitals; or
* worked with clients in a mental institution.

Why? Because Don and his team defined their ministry before they ever started. They didn't try to do too much and were able to work effectively with the groups they concentrated on.

The primary motivations for any puppet ministry are to encourage Christians in their faith and to share Christ with others. But other reasons can also encourage you to start a puppet ministry in your church, such as

* involving children and adults in a relational, hands-on ministry;
* reaching out to the community;
* training volunteers to share their faith; or
* enhancing existing church programs.

Although any puppet team can do all these things to some degree, no team can do everything—all the time. That's why you and your team need to develop a mission statement for your ministry. Pray extensively with your team. Have team members decide exactly what the puppet ministry will look like and what it'll do. Discuss your mission with your puppeteers and church leaders. Guide your team in determining *why* the ministry exists, then compose a mission statement that'll help you accomplish that "why." See the "Sample Mission Statement" below.

Post your team's mission statement prominently in your church, so you'll all be constantly reminded of your purpose and have less chance of being sidetracked by less important things.

• •

Sample Mission Statement

The Praise-Hands puppet team exists to encourage Christians in their faith and to share the gospel with non-Christians.

• •

Your Role as Director

Once your team has defined your puppet ministry mission statement, you're ready to dig in to the week-to-week workings of a puppet ministry team—almost. Before you race off in a mad frenzy to purchase puppets and set up a rehearsal schedule, let's look at your role as the director of this exciting new ministry.

The puppet ministry's success depends largely on the director's enthusiasm, commitment, and organization. It's your job to motivate the team members and helpers and keep the ministry on track. And just how do you do that? Consider these simple tips:

Maintain a positive attitude. Enthusiasm is contagious! One of the best ways to keep your group excited is to keep yourself excited. Pray daily, thanking God for what he has done in your puppet ministry. And tell the team often why you're thankful for them.

Encourage your team members. Volunteers get worn down every day—at work, with their families, even at church. So make puppet rehearsal an encouraging time for the team. Don't overly criticize the team performance at rehearsal. A simple rule to follow is to say ten positive things about a puppeteer's performance for every criticism.

Build relationships. Puppetry isn't the only thing in your team members' lives. Take time to get to know the team members, learn about their interests, and talk with them about their problems. Be available to them. Invite individual team members out occasionally.

Strive for excellence. No one wants to be embarrassed about what he or she does. So push your team to do its best. The team will take more pride in what it's doing.

Pace your workload. Discouragement often comes when there's too much to do and not enough time to do it. Keep track of team members' schedules, and avoid having team members memorize long scripts while they're busy with holidays or with other events. Allow plenty of rehearsal time before each performance.

Have fun. Puppetry is sometimes hard work, but it never has to be boring. Design fun into your rehearsals. Include games, refreshments, and free time. Even have parties after the rehearsals.

A Question of Money

Many ingredients of puppet ministry—puppets, stage, sound equipment, CDs and scripts—require money. So to keep your new puppet ministry afloat, you need a financial plan.

You can usually adjust a puppet ministry's cost to fit your budget. For example, you can purchase materials for a stage, or you can improvise with temporary or simplified stages. Likewise, you can purchase printed scripts, recorded scripts, or songs designed specifically for puppets to perform. Or you can write your own scripts and record them yourselves.

Don't feel you must purchase every item immediately. Begin small and build slowly as the Holy Spirit and your money allow.

Check these options to raise funds for your new puppet ministry:

Fund-raisers—Many puppet groups do fund-raisers and establish a "puppet fund" to pay for supplies. Carwashes, bake sales, even "puppet-thons" (teams puppeteering for long hours) are effective fund-raisers.

Church budget item—Some church budgets allocate money each year for puppet ministry. If you draw up a long-term ministry plan and present it to your church board, you may find that your church would be pleased to support an ongoing puppet ministry.

Gifts and donations—Often individuals or families will gladly support a puppet ministry financially. Get permission from your church to send a letter to all the members explaining what puppet ministry is about and how they can help.

Puppet adoption—Many churches use an "Adopt a Puppet" program to raise money. First, make or purchase one puppet. Then use this puppet in a church service to make an announcement challenging families, individuals, Sunday school classes, or other groups to donate enough money to make or purchase other puppets.

When the first benefactor agrees to donate the required money, publish his or her name in the church bulletin. When the new puppet arrives, take a picture of the new puppet and its sponsor. Then give the sponsor a "Certificate of Adoption."

This approach can also encourage other groups in the church to sponsor puppets. Suggest that church groups follow themes in the adoption process. For example, the senior adult group could adopt a "grandpa" and "grandma" puppet, or a missions group could sponsor multicultural puppets.

Paid performances—After a puppet team has mastered basic puppetry techniques and developed a repertoire, take opportunities to perform outside the church. In many of these situations, your group may receive love offerings or honorariums. Use the gifts to finance future puppet projects.

◆　　◆　　◆　　◆　　◆

Starting a puppet team in your church requires a great deal of thought and prayer, and a willingness to commit your time and energy to a worthwhile cause. As you recruit others to join the puppet team, share your vision with them about the team's future and the possibilities for ministry. Then work together to make your puppet team all that it can be.

UMPH - Uniting r Master's Puppet Hand

Your Puppet Team's Name

Now that your wheels are turning, and your puppet ministry is starting to take shape, you will want to give your team a name. This is a very important step…don't take it lightly! Try to choose a name with a spiritual meaning, but not so "churchy" as to be offensive. For example, the "Hell Fire and Brimstone Gang" name probably would not open very many doors for you. Try to come up with a name that has a double meaning or a "stealth" name that has special meaning to the Christian but is not offensive to the unchurched world. Peruse this list of team names from across the country. Perhaps they will spark your creativity.

- Everlasting Arms
- H.O.P.E. (Helping Our Puppets Evangelize)
- Hands to Heaven
- Feet to Faith
- P.I.G.S. (Puppets In God's Service)
- Hands for Jesus
- The JOY Company
- Glory Fingers
- Holy Hands
- Friendship Connection
- Power Surge
- P.B.J. Puppets (Powered by Jesus)
- Puppet Power

- On Our Knees
- Young Fishers of Men
- Reachin' Teachin' Preachin' Hands
- Master's Hands
- C.I.A. (Christians In Action)
- V.I.P. (Victory in Puppetry)
- H.I.S. Puppet Team
  (Hands in Service)
- Heaven's Handful
- Reignbow Kids
- Lighthouse Puppeteers
- Children of Light

By the way, avoid the word *Muppet* in your puppet team's name, or when describing the puppets you use. *Muppet* is a copyrighted name belonging to Jim Henson Productions. Henson coined the term in 1955 to describe his moving-mouth puppet creations such as Kermit the Frog and Miss Piggy.

   Once you choose your team's name, you might want to create T-shirts, sweatshirts, or team jackets adorned with your team's name and logo. This creates team spirit and builds excitement and identity for your team. Be sure to use artwork that is original or that you have permission for using. If you find artwork in a clip-art book or other commercially available puppet resource, be sure you have permission for its use according to the use statement in the front of the book or from the publisher of that artwork.

CHAPTER 3

The Puppet Family Tree

N ow that you've recruited a puppet ministry team, you're ready to think about the tools of your new trade: puppets. People often assume that "puppets" refers to certain foam rubber creations similar to Jim Henson's Muppet family. But that's just one kind of puppet in the puppet family tree. Several other types can be used by your puppet team, depending on your interests, needs, audience, and message.

Introducing the Family

Churches have used all of the seven general puppet types in their ministries. Let's meet a representative from each limb of the family tree.

Meet Shadow. One of the oldest family members is the shadow puppet. Elaborate shadow puppets have a long history in the Orient and many other parts of the world. All of us have experimented with forming shadows on a screen by making simple hand movements to create a rabbit, a bird, or any number of fun creatures. An audience never actually sees this puppet but enjoys the image on a screen. Puppeteers manipulate and move the puppet to simulate live action. Shadow puppets are great for adding variety to a program and are best adapted to scenes of thinking, dreaming, or flashback; as background characters; or even as figures telling a complete story.

Shadow puppets are inexpensive and easy to make because they are two-dimensional characters. They can be cut from heavy tagboard; leather; or junk materials such as plastic, foam, or cardboard. Moving parts can be added by connecting separate puppet pieces with sticks or wires. A simple attachment overlaps the moving part to the main body of the puppet with a paper fastener or even carpet thread knotted on both sides. The moving part then has a stick or wire attached to it that allows the puppeteer to manipulate that moving piece.

Shadow puppets work by holding the puppets between a strong light source—such as a 150 watt bulb or an overhead projector—and a translucent screen. As the figure is held in front of the light or placed directly on the overhead projector surface, it casts a shadow on the screen. The screen can be something as simple as a muslin sheet stretched tightly or an inexpensive white shower-curtain liner attached to a frame which likewise holds it tightly in place.

Shadow puppets that are placed directly on the surface of an overhead projector will naturally be enlarged by the projector. If a puppeteer wants to place the shadow puppet against the screen and manipulate it from there, the puppet will appear exactly the same size through the screen. Such puppets are therefore usually designed much bigger than those manipulated on the overhead.

The most common shadow puppets project black images on a white screen. However, with creative use of theatrical gels, color transparencies, and other transparent markers or paints, the use of color can be introduced into shadows, with very pleasing effects. Certainly this family member has lots of potential for performance, alone or with other members of the puppet family.

Meet Handy. This simple puppet comes to life when an index finger is placed in the puppet's head and the thumb and middle finger become the puppet's arms. It can pick up small objects easily and express a wide range of emotions. However, it is relatively small and works best with smaller audiences. The absence of a moving mouth makes this puppet ideal for whispering. The performer holding the puppet reacts and relates that conversation to the audience. Fun examples include a rabbit in a hat or a clown popping out of a colorful bag. The puppet might perform magic tricks or retrieve items from the container from which he appeared, lending assistance to the storyteller who is holding the puppet. Without a moving mouth, the *action* becomes more important than the words to depict meaning and emotion.

Behind the stage this puppet can interact with other hand puppets in strong action stories. Many young children find this puppet easy to hold up and manipulate. Simple hand-puppet heads can be constructed with plastic foam, papier-mâché, or some other material and attached to a cloth body—similar to a glove—that fits over the hand.

By the way, don't overlook the power of the human hand acting alone. With the movement and expressive capabilities of four fingers and a thumb, a human hand can communicate complex thoughts, ideas—even humor! The hand can don a white glove and present sign language under a black light. Two hands can also work together for the same effect.

In addition, a hand on either side of a stage might become a pair of "stage hands" bringing props, bowing after the work is done, or clapping after the performance. Hands can also become walking creatures, meeting each other, expressing emotions, or reacting to one another as puppets on stage. Creativity unlocks many doors for these expressive tools.

Meet Rod. The rod puppet consists of a puppet figure supported by a single stick or pole held from below. Other rods can be attached to arms or legs for gestures or additional movements.

Simple characters such as bees or butterflies lend themselves to this type of puppet. However, complicated puppets can also be constructed by adding strings or wires to additional moving parts. Often objects such as mops, brooms, or yardsticks can become unique puppet characters through the addition of eyes, ears, mouths, and other character parts.

Meet Mari. An action story with two or more characters moving in and out of the scene lends itself to the marionette style of puppetry. The entire puppet body is visible to the audience, and a skilled puppeteer manipulates strings attached to the puppet to cause it to perform human-like movements.

Marionettes require a stage built especially for them. Hence, this type of puppet doesn't mix well with the other family members.

Marionette manipulation requires great finger dexterity and practice, and it is considered more difficult than other types of puppetry. Simple marionettes may be made and used by children, but the more advanced, complicated types require much more skill to make and manipulate.

Meet Woody. A popular puppet in the puppet family tree is the ventriloquist's partner—sometimes called a dummy. Humor is its trademark, and illusion is the key to its success. In ventriloquism, a puppeteer brings a puppet to life while he or she remains in full view of the audience. The puppeteer, or ventriloquist, must create a distinct character voice for his or her "vent-pal," give the audience the illusion that the character is speaking totally on its own, focus his or her attention on the puppet, and avoid all lip movement and facial gestures while the puppet is talking.

Generally a ventriloquist works with only one puppet at a time; some performers have mastered the voices and manipulation of two characters simultaneously carrying on a conversation with the ventriloquist. The traditional ventriloquist puppet is a carved wooden figure. The wood characters usually have mouth and eye movements with additional facial movements possible, all operated from a control stick in the back of the puppet. Many ventriloquists are now using a soft foam-and-cloth full-bodied puppet instead of a wooden figure. Soft puppets typically have only a moving mouth, but there are more of them created now with other moving parts as well.

This family member is a great character to use in transitions for a complete puppet program. The ventriloquist can come out in front of the stage to perform while the puppeteers behind the stage are preparing for the next segment.

Meet Mouthy. The moving-mouth hand puppet has become the most popular puppet type, owing much of its success to TV programs such as *Sesame Street, Between the Lions,* and *Bear in the Big Blue House.*

A moving-mouth hand puppet typically is a half-bodied puppet with stuffed arms made mobile by attaching a rod to each wrist. One of the puppeteer's hands fits into the mouth of the puppet, which opens once for each syllable spoken by the puppet. The puppeteer's other hand operates one or both rods attached to the arms in order to make the puppet more lifelike.

Because the mouth must be opened and closed for each syllable of each word, these puppets require more hand and arm strength and physical effort than any other type. They're also more difficult to construct than some types. However, this type of puppet can express a wide array of emotions and movements, which makes it ideal for many puppet teams.

Meet Holder. Holder is a moving-mouth puppet that has special sleeves and gloves designed for the puppeteer to put his or her hands into so objects can be held and manipulated. That is why this family member has been called a *human-hand puppet.* Movements such as pointing, counting with the fingers, directing music, holding drumsticks or other musical instruments, sign language, and clapping are made easy with human-hand puppets. This type of puppet is quite capable of holding even fairly heavy objects and can do many things impossible for other styles of puppets.

When the human-hand puppet is operated by one puppeteer, the puppeteer puts one hand in the puppet's head and one hand in a sleeve and glove. The second (unused) sleeve and glove can be stuffed and pinned to the puppet's body in a casual position.

When two puppeteers are used, one puppeteer operates the head while the second puppeteer operates both of the hands. Usually the taller puppeteer manipulates the head while kneeling behind the shorter "hands" person.

Choosing Your Puppets

Before you spend time making puppets or investing in ready-made ones, decide which puppet type best fits your team's needs. Most puppet teams choose the moving-mouth hand puppets because of their versatility and durability. Also, volunteers can learn to manipulate these puppets more quickly than they could a marionette or a complicated rod puppet.

If you use moving-mouth hand puppets as the foundation of your puppet ensemble, include a few shadow puppets or rod puppets to add variety to your program and give your puppeteers an added challenge.

In the beginning, choose moving-mouth hand puppets that adapt well to a variety of scripts and songs. For example, a boy moving-mouth hand puppet can be costumed as a grandpa or a biblical character. But a bird or dog puppet can't be used for anything other than what it is. Use animal characters as emcees, storytellers, or in other special roles.

Some puppet characters are designed so that the eyes, nose, ears, and hair can be removed and reattached with Velcro. This seems great until you remember that any feature that's removable is also losable! Still, you may want puppets with removable clothing and hair so they can easily take on other roles.

Caring for Your Tools

In puppet ministry, your puppets and props are your tools. And whether you've purchased your puppets or made them, they represent a sizable investment of time and money. Because of this, special care must be taken to store and transport puppets to keep them in good condition.

Since most puppets are made of fabric and foam, they can become soiled or damaged unless cared for properly. When puppets are new, spray them with a fabric protector. If you get a dirty spot or stain on the puppet, surface wash the soiled area with a mild spot remover or fabric cleaner.

Puppeteers must be carefully trained to take care of the puppets. Here are some do's and don'ts to help you lengthen your puppets' lives:

Do

- Store puppets in a box or trunk away from dust, dampness, or unsupervised children.
- Remove the rods when packing puppets into boxes. Place puppets with faces toward the inside, away from the box surface.
- Treat puppets as if they're very fragile—they are!
- Brush a puppet's hair before each entrance.
- Visually check the overall appearance of the puppet before it enters the performance stage, including hair, clothing, hats, accessories, and arm position.

Don't

- Leave puppets lying around on the floor where people will step on them.
- Pack puppets too tightly. That will smash the puppets.
- Pick puppets up by the hair, nose, or ears—ouch!
- Bite *anything* with the mouth of a puppet. Doing so will bend, break, and eventually ruin the cardboard stiffener in the puppet's mouth.
- Allow puppeteers to bang puppets together.
- Allow puppeteers to eat or drink while working with puppets. Greasy hands and spilled drinks are dangerous to your puppets' health.

Now that you've met all the members of the puppet family tree and know how to care for your puppets, you're ready to focus on effective puppet manipulation techniques. We'll concentrate our efforts on the moving-mouth hand puppet since that's the most common type of puppet used in puppet ministry. However, the ideas presented will be helpful for any style of puppetry your ministry may tackle.

Buying vs. Sewing

Puppets are the centerpiece of your puppet ministry. Therefore, they need to be top-quality products. But that doesn't always mean lots of money. You can purchase ready-made puppets from a puppet supply company, or you can create them from commercial patterns:

Buying

ADVANTAGES

- ◆ You can usually get the puppets quickly.
- ◆ You'll get professional-quality puppets.
- ◆ They'll usually last longer than hand-made puppets.
- ◆ You can see what you're getting.

DISADVANTAGES

- ◆ Puppets cost more initially.
- ◆ Your puppets will look similar to other groups' puppets.
- ◆ You must plan your skits in advance to get the puppets you'll need.
- ◆ Sometimes ready-made puppets are stiff and difficult to manipulate.

Sewing

ADVANTAGES

- ◆ Puppets cost less.
- ◆ You can create unique characters.
- ◆ You can personalize your puppets.
- ◆ You have total control over costuming, skin color, size, and type.

DISADVANTAGES

- ◆ You must find a good pattern with clear directions.
- ◆ It usually takes more time.
- ◆ It often takes several attempts to create a quality puppet.
- ◆ Materials are sometimes hard to find.

Whatever puppets you choose, make sure they're worthy of representing your church and the purpose of your ministry. Don't use any puppets your puppeteers are ashamed to be seen with!

Emergency! Emergency!

When a doctor goes on a house call, he takes every tool or instrument he might need. When a plumber comes to fix your plumbing, he brings the tools he needs to complete the job.

So it makes sense that a puppet team carry a "tool" box to every practice and performance to take care of minor emergencies without wasting time and energy.

Many teams use a fishing tackle box or carpenter's toolbox because of the many little storage compartments.

Use this checklist when stocking your puppet team's toolbox:

❑ adhesive bandages

❑ small hammer

❑ hot glue gun and glue sticks

❑ utility knife

❑ duct tape

❑ upholstery pins

❑ razor blades

❑ needle and thread

❑ extension cords

❑ stapler

❑ safety pins

❑ spare gloves for human-hand puppets

❑ pliers

❑ scissors

❑ T-pins

❑ ruler

❑ transparent tape

❑ screwdrivers (Phillips and regular)

❑ thumbtacks

❑ straight pins

❑ black marker

❑ rubber bands

❑ spare eyes for puppets

❑ three-prong plug adapters

In addition to these items, carry business cards or copies of a small brochure about your puppet ministry. If you do a sharp program, you'll have people from the audience wanting to book you for an engagement at their church or organization.

CHAPTER 4

Bringing Puppets to Life

A good puppeteer can make a foam and fabric object become a believable, attention-getting character. The puppet is an actor, and the puppeteer controls the actor's movements. But making a puppet come to life on stage isn't easy. The skills puppeteers need to project a character through a puppet require time, practice, and, most of all, attention to detail. Puppeteers need to learn the techniques "right the first time" so the skills they need will eventually come naturally.

Standing in the Spotlight

A puppet's movements and position are critical to the success of the character you're portraying. Examine these basic puppet manipulation techniques each of your puppeteers must learn.

Entering and exiting—You want the puppet to appear to walk into and out of view. To accomplish this, face the front of the stage, reach back behind your head, and "walk" the puppet up four or five imaginary stairs toward the stage. From the audience's view, the puppet is walking toward the front of the stage and "up the stairs" into full view.

To exit, just reverse the procedure, turning the puppet's back to the stage and walking it down and away from the audience in the same stair-step motion.

While your moving-mouth hand puppet is on stage, your arm should be extended straight up from your shoulder. Don't bend your elbow except during the entrance and exit. If you attempt to perform with a bent elbow, your puppet's height will vary greatly and your arm will tire quickly.

Height and positioning—After the puppet has entered into view of the audience, the audience shouldn't see the puppeteer's arm. Nor should people see just the puppet's head. The proper height is "belly button" level. If the puppet had a belly button, it would be even with the top of the stage. Be sure to maintain that same height, not allowing the puppet to sink during performance or make sudden jerks upward to get back to that correct height. No quicksand or potholes should seem to appear as the puppets are performing.

Keep the puppet at least eight inches back from the front of the stage to allow room for arm movements and other actions. And allow a comfortable distance between the faces of your puppets so they are positioned for normal conversation.

Lip synchronization—The moving-mouth hand puppet requires precise manipulation to make the mouth movement seem realistic. In general, open the puppet's mouth once for each syllable of spoken words, and close it between the syllables or when the puppet isn't talking.

For example, to say "hello," open the puppet's mouth twice. To say "My name is Bobby," open the puppet's mouth five times— once for each syllable.

When making a puppet speak, a beginning puppeteer will commonly "flip the lid" of the puppet (move the top part of the puppet's head) for each syllable. This makes the puppet throw its head back every time it speaks. With practice, though, any puppeteer can learn to lower the puppet's jaw instead of flip its lid. That way the puppet maintains proper eye contact with the audience.

Another common error is to open the puppet's mouth as wide as possible every time it speaks. If the puppet is whispering or speaking softly, open the mouth just a little. If the puppet is talking normally, open the mouth one-third to one-half of the way. If the puppet is yawning, yelling, or singing loudly, open the mouth to its fullest extent.

Eye contact and head position—When a puppet speaks to the audience, the head should be tipped down a bit so that the focus of the eyes will be toward the faces of the audience. When a puppet speaks to another puppet on the stage, his head should turn toward that puppet, and the focus of his eyes should be toward the other character. This focus must be learned and can be improved by having a director sit in front of the stage, giving appropriate feedback to the puppeteers as they rehearse. Other specific action in the puppet performance might require the puppet to look up or in other directions. Puppet director feedback is the best tool for learning appropriate movements.

Believable action and reaction—When a puppet moves across the stage, it should appear to be walking. To do that, the puppet will move with "bouncelike" steps rather than float across the stage. Each character should move in believable ways. An old man will walk more slowly than a young child, and a flower should not walk at all but could grow up and wilt down as it enters and exits the stage. As the characters perform, they will also react to things said or done to them during the performance. It is vitally important to keep the puppets moving believably throughout the presentation. Wild, uncontrolled head bobbing or standing on stage like a statue is not pleasing to the audience and usually distracts from the message of the performance.

Making All the Right Moves

When the puppets are "standing" at the correct height on stage, maintaining eye contact with the audience and even moving their mouths in sync with the tape, the learning has just begun. Puppeteers must still learn to make all the puppets' movements believable.

Rod-arm puppet movements—Attaching a rod to one of the puppet's arms greatly increases the range of movement possible for that puppet. Attach the rod to the puppet's left wrist if the puppeteer is right-handed, or vice versa. Then practice using the puppet's arm to express these actions:

- Scratch head.
- Rub eyes.
- Yawn.
- Take a bow.
- Cough.
- Rub tummy.
- Throw kisses.
- Look into the distance.
- Sneeze.
- Do a double take.

- Show concentration.
- Show excitement.
- Express fear.

- Express sadness.
- Pretend to be hard of hearing.

Once you've mastered lip-sync with one rod attached, try two-handed movements with rods attached to both arms. Keep in mind that not all movements require both arms. You will often use one rod at a time even though both arms have rods attached.

When using two rods together, there are several ways to hold them for maximum control. Experiment with each method to see what works best for you or for the action you are trying to create. The most common technique is to cross the rods in an X, holding the tops of the rods between your thumb and index finger while slipping your little finger between the rods at the bottom of the X. See the illustration on page 38. A second method is to "palm" the bottoms of both rods in your hand and raise the arms high over the head of the puppet. See the illustration on page 38. A third technique is to grab both rods tightly together, holding the wooden handles side by side as you employ a pinching movement to the two rods for puppet arm movement. See the illustration on page 39.

Experiment with the various two-rod holding methods to create the following moves:

- Clap hands.
- Play peekaboo.
- Sneeze.
- Blow nose.
- Have a coughing fit.

- Pray.
- Fly like an airplane.
- Run in place.
- Do jumping jacks.

Human-arm puppet movements—Human-arm puppets require cooperation between two puppeteers. The puppeteers' positioning is awkward and requires stamina. Use these procedures when training puppeteers to operate a two-handed human-arm puppet:

- One puppeteer operates the head, while the other puppeteer operates both the puppet's hands.
- The taller puppeteer operates the head.
- The "head" operator stands behind the "hands" operator.
- The hands operator kneels on both knees. The head operator kneels on one knee between the legs of the hands operator.

- The puppet's body stays ten to twelve inches away from the stage to give the hands room to operate.
- The hands always drop out of sight before the puppet moves from one location to another.

To practice believable actions for the one-handed human-arm puppet, use the list of actions for the single-rod-arm puppet. For the two-handed human-arm puppet, try these movements:

- Read a Bible.
- Cover face.
- Bite fingernails.
- Clap.
- Throw paper wads.
- Direct a song.
- Sit down and think.
- Blow nose.
- Run in place.

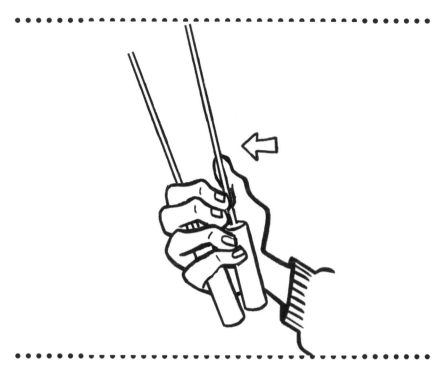

Dressing the Part

Some say "clothes make the man," and it's certainly true that costuming can work wonders in helping your puppets come alive! Use these suggestions to improve your puppetry through costuming.

Collect hats. Use cowboy hats, Jewish skullcaps, turbans, women's hats, Chinese hats, Indian feathers or headdresses, police hats, firefighter hats, construction worker hats, baseball hats, visors—any hats that convey certain characters or moods. Find them in secondhand stores or toy shops. Also, Halloween is an excellent time to pick up unique hats and other costume items.

Collect toddlers' clothes. The best puppetry costuming can often be found in your neighbor's garage. Sizes 2 to 4 work best. Also collect cloth scraps to use as puppet accessories such as scarves or headbands.

When using costumes or other props, make sure they are

securely attached to the puppet. Nothing damages a puppet play as much as costuming falling off or flopping around. Avoid this by sewing costuming directly on the puppets. Or use safety pins, upholstery pins, or Velcro.

Creating Character Through Voice

So your puppet looks good and moves in a convincing manner. But what happens when your puppet must speak?

Puppets are fantasy figures. They look similar to cartoons. And their voices should reflect what they are. Puppet voices should appeal to the audience and be easily understood. But they should also have a cartoon-character quality. Puppet voices can be categorized into six basic voice qualities:

1. Whispered—Use your own voice but add a strong whisper over it at all times.
2. Nasal—Exaggerate the "n" sound behind all your words, squeezing the air through your nose as you talk.
3. Goofy—Drop the pitch, slow the tempo, and move into the mind-set of "Duh, I dunno."
4. Guttural—Use a rolling "r" behind all your words to convey harshness or to make animal sounds such as a dog's growl or a lion's roar.
5. Falsetto—Talk about an octave above your regular pitch.
6. Melodic—Almost sing the words and add a rich vibrato. Give your words an operatic feel.

You can create scores of characters from these six basic voices by experimenting with other elements of sound.

- Pitch—how high or low the tone of the voice sounds. For example, a little girl would have a high voice, while a football player would have a low voice.
- Volume—how softly or loudly a character speaks. For example, a country farmer might speak loudly, while a shy boy might speak quietly.
- Tempo—how fast or slowly the character speaks. For example, a mouse character might rattle words off quickly, while a turtle would speak slowly.
- Diction—how a word is pronounced. For example, a city puppet might pronounce nothing "nuh-thing," but a rural

puppet might say "nut-tin."

◆ Word choice—how words are chosen to fit the character
you're creating. For example, a grandpa puppet might say
"young-uns," while a child puppet might say "kids."

◆ ◆ ◆ ◆ ◆

Encourage your puppeteers to be patient as they learn correct
puppet manipulation techniques. Have volunteers practice them
every time you rehearse. Taking time to learn these techniques in
the early stages of your puppet ministry will save you time later.
And good skills, when combined with creative costuming and
fun voice effects, will heighten puppeteers' enjoyment and
increase your ministry's effectiveness.

CHAPTER 5

Designing a Program

Whated hen architects design a building, they always consider the area's climate. A building built in Anchorage, Alaska, for instance, would be quite different from one in Key West, Florida.

Planning performance material works much the same way. The material you select needs to fit the "climate"—or audience. Puppets can be used effectively with all types of audiences. Teenagers, elementary kids, adults, preschoolers, and senior citizens can all join in the fun of puppetry.

Puppetry can also be done in different settings, such as public parks, malls, hospitals, even prisons.

With properly chosen material, puppetry can entertain and inspire people in any of these audiences or settings. Let's consider how puppetry could be used effectively in each of these audiences and settings.

Preschoolers—Young children have a short attention span, so avoid any play that's more than three minutes long. Songs should also be short and familiar so children can sing along. Use several different puppets throughout the performance, and have the puppets interact with the kids as much as possible.

Elementary kids—Children are always an eager audience for puppet songs and skits. Current Christian musicals for children can often be done with puppets. Skits should be kept short, lasting no longer than five minutes.

Puppet plays can consist of Bible stories, modern adaptations of

Bible stories, or topical skits with a biblical message kids can understand.

One technique that works well with children is to use a real person—such as one of the puppeteers—in front of the stage to interact with a puppet. This helps maintain audience control and attention.

Teenagers—Young people like puppets for the same reasons other people do: They're fun, they remind us of childhood, and they entertain us with their often wild antics.

Teenagers almost always enjoy puppets, but especially when they do skits that deal with teenage issues or relationships. Use material that contains teenage lingo or parodies of popular teenage idols. Rewrite Bible stories using modern characters and situations, getting the same truth across.

Skits focusing on family problems can also be effective. For example, act out a tense conflict between a father and son, then interview each character individually to get his side of the story. From there, launch a discussion with the audience, having them suggest possible resolutions. You might want to have the puppets act out the audience's suggestions.

Adults—Adults enjoy takeoffs on current TV shows, well-known personalities, or popular songs. Material for adults should contain humor yet effectively hit on issues adults deal with daily. With puppets you can tackle touchy subjects—like giving, honesty, and church participation—more easily than a pastor can.

Senior citizens—This audience prefers relatively slow, familiar, easy-to-understand songs. They'll also enjoy the children's songs they sang as kids.

Use grandpa and grandma puppet characters to talk about Bible stories or the more recent past. Allow the audience to interact with the puppets—have puppets tell jokes, ask questions, or just reminisce with the audience.

Public parks and malls—People in these settings are usually on their way somewhere and have little time to spare. Therefore, design a clever, action-packed program that will grab their attention. Keep segments short, to the point, and suitable for adults as well as children. Lively puppet songs coupled with a capable "out front" person work well in this situation. Remember to secure permission from the mall manager or park supervisor and follow the facility's guidelines.

Hospitals and prisons—These audiences each are unique, so take special care to talk to a representative of the institution about the type of audience you're dealing with. Discuss your performance segments to be certain the things you choose to perform are appropriate.

Put yourself in the audience's place and evaluate your material as if you were one of them. Be sensitive to the special needs and background of each person in your audience.

Choosing Your Material

No matter who your audience is, you'll want material with a message. However, you'll also want some "just for fun" material to provide comic relief and add interest to the program.

Guidelines for developing a program differ depending on whether you're performing live or from recorded material, as well as whether you want a musical or a drama. Let's look at each of these options:

Live material—For live performances, stick with skits that have only two or three characters and are less than five minutes long. Long, live productions can be tiresome—both for the puppeteers and for the audience. Cut longer programs into several three- to five-minute segments, with fun narratives or vignettes between.

When choosing skits to perform as live material, ask yourself these questions:

- Do we have puppeteers who can project their voices effectively or do we have needed sound equipment?
- Do we have puppeteers who can create voices to match the characters in the skit?
- Do we have enough puppeteers to do all the voices, or will some puppeteers have to do more than one voice?
- Does the skit have any hard-to-memorize speeches?

Recorded material—Choose recorded skits that sound professional yet not "canned." Also consider the skit's message and story line to determine what audiences you could use it with. Avoid skits that have only limited usefulness. For example, a Christmas skit aimed at senior citizens can likely be used only once or twice.

When choosing prerecorded puppet skits, ask yourself these questions:

+ Are the words intelligible?
+ Are the lines short, concise, and not "preachy"?
+ Are there only two or three characters on stage at a time?
+ Are extravagant sets and props required?
+ Is there enough time for entrances, exits, and scene changes?
+ Is any one character on stage for more than five minutes at a time?

Your Performance Style

A major consideration in puppet ministry is deciding whether to perform live or with recorded material. There ar e many advantages to each approach. Let's take a look at a few of them.

ADVANTAGES OF LIVE MATERIAL

+ You can tailor your program to a specific audience more easily.
+ You can interact with the audience more easily.
+ You can react to unexpected problems or audience response.
+ You can shorten or lengthen your skit.

DISADVANTAGES OF LIVE MATERIAL

+ The puppeteer must work with a microphone.
+ The puppeteer must change his or her voice for different characters and speak clearly and distinctly.
+ Live songs usually don't work as well as prerecorded ones.

ADVANTAGES OF RECORDED MATERIAL

+ An abundance of puppet songs and skits is available.
+ You can use music and sound effects you can't do live.
+ The result sounds more professional.
+ You can have special voices your puppeteers may not be able to do.

DISADVANTAGES OF RECORDED MATERIAL

+ You may encounter technical difficulties.
+ Sometimes the program sounds canned.
+ More rehearsal time is needed to memorize the timing.
+ Recorded performing prevents interaction with the audience.

Programming for One

In addition to programs designed for entire puppet teams, you can also "go solo" with puppets, using them to interact with groups or just to entertain. Check out these three ideas for using puppets to help you lead or interact with your group:

PUPPET SPECIALS—Select a song that fits the theme of an upcoming meeting. Then send a puppet and a CD of the song home with an interested volunteer. Ask him or her to practice the song and be ready to perform it for the group on the appropriate week. Don't worry if the puppetry isn't perfect—volunteers will enjoy seeing a peer make the attempt.

STORY TIME—Use a puppet character to tell stories that relate to the meeting theme each week. Make the stories silly and lighthearted. Kids may laugh and joke, but don't let that discourage you. The story's message will still get through.

DRAMA MOPS—For a twist on storytelling time, give some of the kids mops and brooms, and have them create rod puppets. Encourage kids to use anything they can find—paper, cloth, wire, or whatever—to create faces and costumes for the mops and brooms.

Have kids with puppets kneel behind a partition in front of the class. Tell a story and have puppeteers act it out as you speak. This is great fun for the kids and provides a creative way to get your point across.

Puppet songs—When choosing songs for your puppets to sing, consider these suggestions:

- Match the number of voices on the tape to the number of puppets you use. Avoid the "choir" sound whenever possible.
- Make sure the audience will be able to understand the words.
- Choose lively songs. The greatest puppeteers in the world would have trouble keeping an audience awake if the songs put them to sleep.
- Pick songs that have a purpose. This doesn't necessarily mean a spiritual message. Perhaps you want the song to entertain or to make the audience laugh. That's OK. What's important is that the song has a specific, positive effect on the audience.

- Choose songs that can be choreographed. Think of how costuming, props, or special effects could enhance the song's message.
- Match the type of song with the puppets you're using. For example, a black gospel arrangement won't work well if you have only white puppets.

Complete musical productions—Several complete musicals have been written for puppets. They're similar to choir musicals, but include stage directions and characters better fitted to puppet ministry. Productions like these work well for puppet teams that go on tour or perform the same production many times in their area.

When considering a full-length musical production with puppets, consider these questions:

- Can the puppet team physically handle a thirty- to forty-minute presentation?
- Is this musical's spiritual message worth your effort, time, and expense?
- Do the musical styles vary, or do all the songs sound the same?
- Is there a meaningful story line between the songs?
- Does the musical require certain characters to stay on stage for long periods? If so, would it be possible to switch puppeteers to provide a rest for overworked arms?
- Could the youth choir or children's choir sing the songs and the puppets do only the drama segments?

Putting It All Together

After you've learned the basics of puppet manipulation, selected songs and skits to work on, and got a few practices behind you, it won't be long before you're called on to perform.

Don't panic! Putting a program together really isn't all that hard. Begin by answering these two questions:

1. What type of audience is it?
2. How long does the program need to be?

Once you answer these two questions, scan the skits and songs you've worked on and decide whether any are appropriate for this performance.

If so, you're in good shape. If not, ask yourself if you have enough time to prepare new material. If not, turn down the invitation— instead of performing inappropriate material or poorly rehearsed songs and skits.

If you do have time to prepare a new program, where do you begin? Here are some steps to take:

Develop a theme. Whatever audience or program length you have, you need a theme for your presentation. A theme can focus on a Bible verse, a biblical truth such as forgiveness, a virtue such as honesty, or a relational issue such as making friends or getting along with Mom and Dad. Holiday themes also work well if the timing is right.

Tie the segments together. A puppet presentation usually contains several segments, such as recorded puppet songs, live Bible verses, live or recorded puppet skits, and puppet interaction with the audience. Each of these segments must fit together smoothly with an effective transition or "bridge." One of the best ways to build this bridge is with a narrator puppet that carries the audience from one scene to the next. The narrator tells a story, sings a song, interacts with the audience, or just explains what's coming up next.

Using a bridge character has two advantages:
- It gives the puppeteers time to switch positions backstage and to change or dress puppets.
- It provides a way to connect the segments to your theme.

Even if your collection of skits and songs seems disjointed, you can usually pull it together around a theme by using a bridge character throughout the program.

Get feedback. When you perform, always ask your host what he or she thought of the program. Try to get honest criticism. Also ask puppeteers to express their feelings about their performance. Ask them how things are going backstage and what changes or improvements can be made.

Burn Out or Rust Out

Once your puppet ministry is in operation, your team will need to determine how often to perform. If you perform too often— especially the same material over and over—your team members may start to show signs of burnout.

On the other hand, if you practice and practice but never perform, your team may grow restless and discouraged. That condition is often called rustout. And you can correct it only by getting your team in front of an audience more often.

So how often should you perform? No one answer applies to everyone. Some teams perform once or twice a week—and like it that way. Other teams perform once or twice a month. And some spend two or three months rehearsing a full-length musical, which they then perform several times in a matter of days.

You will need to determine the correct spacing of performances for your group. Several factors may affect your performance schedule, such as team members' personal schedules, availability of transportation, and the number of people who can help with putting on a production. Consider these prayerfully as you set the calendar for your puppet team.

◆   ◆   ◆   ◆   ◆

Putting together a program for your puppet team can be a fun, rewarding experience. But it also takes time, energy, and a knack for knowing just what skits or songs will fit a particular audience. It also takes skill to make a variety of skits and songs flow together smoothly as one unified program.

But don't let that discourage you. With a little practice and some positive experiences, you'll soon grow confident of your ability to effectively convey a message through puppets.

CHAPTER 6

Practice Makes Perfect

A puppet ministry team, in many ways, is like a drama group. Participants memorize scripts and movements, develop muscular abilities, and learn to work together as a team.

And that takes practice.

Teams need regular rehearsals to develop the muscular strength, memorization skills, and cooperation needed to master the plays, skits, and songs of puppet ministry. Most puppet teams find meeting for an hour and a half each week is about right.

Successful rehearsals focus on three areas: devotions, communication, and practice. Dividing your puppet rehearsals this way gives you the practice time you need, while not ignoring team members' spiritual growth or relationships. Let's look more closely at each of these areas.

Devotions—Spend time at the beginning of your rehearsal doing a devotion with your volunteers. Encourage team members to talk about their concerns, personal needs, and answers to prayer. Allow team members to take turns leading the devotion time, and encourage volunteers to interact with one another during this time of spiritual refreshment.

See the "Ideas for Rehearsal Devotions" box on page 51 for more insights on ministry with puppeteers.

Ideas for Rehearsal Devotions

Since your puppet team is a ministry to one another as well as a ministry to your audiences, do everything you can to set the tone for ministry by having regular, significant, devotional times at your rehearsals. Consider these suggestions for helping volunteers focus on ministry in puppetry:

◆ Never allow leaders or puppeteers to ridicule or put one another down.

◆ Take time for prayer requests and prayer, showing respect for each person's needs.

◆ Invite church staff members, puppeteer parents, and church and community leaders to come to rehearsal to share testimonies and lead devotions.

◆ Have different puppeteers take turns leading devotionals on topics of their choice.

◆ Spend time on Bible memory verses and singing praise choruses.

◆ Break up into groups of two or three to encourage the sharing of personal concerns and prayer for each other.

◆ Discuss current events, and explore what the Bible says relevant to these current events.

◆ Have each puppeteer choose a favorite recorded song to play for the group, sharing why that song is especially meaningful to him or her.

◆ Select a Christian novel appropriate for the age and spiritual maturity of the group. Read a chapter each week, using the story as a discussion starter.

◆ Visit your Christian bookstore for workbooks and study guides on topics relevant to the needs of your group.

◆ Read a different Bible story each week, and discuss what can be learned from it.

Communication time—As the director, you must regularly communicate details of upcoming performances and allow volunteers to ask questions or express concerns. Encourage puppeteers each to bring a calendar to mark performance dates. Allow about ten to fifteen minutes to discuss upcoming perform-ances and to field questions. Also mail a performance and prac-tice schedule to puppeteers' homes.

Practice time—Spend about one-third of the rehearsal time working on basic techniques such as entering and exiting, lip-sync, rod-arm use, and maintaining proper height. Use the remaining time developing your repertoire of songs and skits for performances. Practice a variety of skits—funny, serious, musical, action-packed, reflective—to keep puppeteers' interest.

Effective Policies

Before diving into a full-blown rehearsal schedule, discuss your team's purposes and goals with your team members, and set up policies to help you reach those goals. Write all the team's policies—concerning attendance, behavior, and church participation—and have team members each sign and date the list. Make sure they understand what's expected of them.

The toughest issue you'll deal with may be regulating rehearsal attendance and absences. Since every puppeteer will have assigned parts, it's vital that you develop a fairly strict attendance policy so rehearsal time stays productive. On the other hand, family demands and unexpected occurrences require some flexibility.

Other areas may also require policy statements. For example, many volunteers have time conflicts between jobs and rehearsals. Think about possible problems you'll encounter, and develop policies to deal with these problems before they occur.

See the "Sample Policy Statement" on page 53 for more ideas.

Productive Planning

Rehearsal time can be fun, productive, and enjoyable—provided you plan your time effectively. Here are twelve hints for making rehearsal time work *for* rather than *against* you.

1. **Hold regular rehearsals.** Set a regular time to practice each week, and don't change it unless absolutely necessary.
2. **Arrive early.** Be there at least thirty minutes before rehearsal time to get everything organized: puppets, props, rods, recorded material, scripts, devotions, and anything else you'll need. Maybe ask a different puppeteer to help you prepare each week.

Sample Policy Statement

FIRST CHURCH OF SOMEWHERE, U.S.A.
MR. AND MRS. PUPPET LEADER, DIRECTORS

1. The puppet team will meet in the sanctuary from 7 to 8:30 p.m. every Tuesday. All puppeteers are required to be on time.
2. Any puppeteer who has to miss a rehearsal or performance <u>for any reason</u> must notify the puppet director as far in advance as possible. Failure to notify the puppet director in advance of any absence may result in temporary suspension from the team.
3. Puppeteers <u>may not</u> bring visitors to rehearsals without prior permission of the director.
4. Excessive absence from puppet practice will result in suspension from the team.
5. Puppeteers will take an active role in deciding on material the team will perform and where the team will perform it.
6. All puppeteers are expected to attend services at First Church regularly. Each puppeteer must attend at least four church services or activities per month in addition to puppet rehearsals.
7. Puppeteers may earn personal credit through participation in fund-raising activities and by performing in extra "paid" performances. This credit remains in the puppetry fund and may be used <u>only</u> toward the annual puppetry tour.

TEAM VERSE
Ecclesiastes 9:10a
"Whatever your hand finds to do, do it with all your might."

3. *Write your rehearsal agenda.* Prepare a schedule of what you want the team to rehearse, as well as a listing of required puppets, recorded material, scripts, props, and assigned parts. This will help you keep on track during rehearsal.
4. *Keep everyone busy.* If your puppeteers sit around all evening, they'll wonder why they're there. If you have too

many people to manage, get more help. One leader can work best with five to eight puppeteers at a time. Have alternative activities ready for puppeteers who aren't directly involved in the skit you're rehearsing. Have them help make costumes, clean puppets, or practice new voices.

5. **Don't get into a rut.** Include something new each week. Let volunteers hear or try out new material. Spend time working on new live voices. Have team members switch parts. Have a party. Watch a video. Go out for fast food—anything to keep rehearsals exciting!

Experiment with these suggestions to avoid the "rehearsal rut":

- Have a Puppet Raid! Take your team to someone's house and do an impromptu skit. You could even show up with all your puppets on your pastor's front porch.
- Have a Puppet Visitation Night, where your puppeteers go to a visitor's house and have the puppets invite that person back to church.
- Plan a Puppet Shopping Spree. Take your puppets to a discount store, and let them try on shirts, hats, or other clothing items. Then purchase the items for your prop box and puppet wardrobe.

6. **Allow time to learn material.** Don't do a forty-minute musical after only two or three rehearsals. After volunteers learn to lip-sync songs or plays, they still must work on staging, choreography, props, and other extras that make the production unique.

7. **Direct from the audience's perspective.** Sit or stand in front of the stage as you direct. Avoid performing unless absolutely necessary. You need to be the "eyes of the audience," and deal with problems in positioning, puppet manipulation, and height during the rehearsal.

8. **Emphasize positive things you see.** Puppeteers need positive reinforcement as well as constructive criticism. Point out the good things you see happening—avoid just pointing out errors.

9. **Encourage puppeteers to learn all the parts.** You never know when illness or an unexpected absence may require you

to switch puppeteers' parts. Encourage puppeteers to pay attention to every part in case changes must be made.

10. *Practice a variety of material.* Rehearse a broad spectrum of material: comic and serious; musical and dramatic; recorded and live; seasonal and non-seasonal. Not only does it keep rehearsals interesting, it also challenges volunteers to stretch their puppeteering abilities.

11. *Take time for fun!* Plan parties, trips, and other fun times. Reward puppeteers for their work and dedication. Sometimes an ice cream cone says much more than a thousand thank yous.

12. *Delegate responsibility to puppeteers.* Team members can do most of the tasks in puppet ministry, such as setting up the stage, gathering puppets and props, grooming puppets, and putting away equipment after rehearsal.

Successful Scheduling

It takes experience to know how much time to rehearse a skit before you perform it. Spending too much time on one piece makes puppetry boring, while not spending enough time can discourage puppeteers. The following steps apply to learning prerecorded material. Learning live material follows a similar path, with time added for script reading and voice development.

1. *Review the material with puppeteers.* Answer questions such as: "What are we doing?" "Why are we doing it?" and "Where will we use it?" Puppeteers need to understand why they're doing a particular piece and how it will be used in ministry.

2. *Play the recorded material.* Have puppeteers read the script as they listen.

3. *Assign parts to puppeteers.* Normally you should decide who should take each part, based on each puppeteer's skill, voice, and present workload.

4. *Play the recording again.* Have puppeteers move their thumbs in sync with the voices on the recording.

5. *Have puppeteers listen to the recording and lip-sync with their puppets.* After a few practice runs, have puppeteers put away their scripts and just follow the recording.

Puppetry Skill Levels

...g volunteers isn't easy. And puppetry requires the kind of long-term dedication that only select volunteers have to give. But you can encourage team members' interest in puppet ministry and keep them striving to do better.

Here's a four-level achievement program to challenge your puppeteers toward excellence in puppetry. Puppeteers must fulfill the requirements listed to achieve each level.

LEVEL ONE—APPRENTICE PUPPETEER

◆ Attend puppet rehearsals regularly for three months.
◆ Learn basic puppet manipulation techniques.
◆ Learn to set up stages and care for the equipment.
◆ Maintain a good attitude toward leaders and other puppeteers.
◆ Participate in six performances, two of which must be away from the church.

LEVEL TWO—JOURNEYMAN PUPPETEER

◆ Complete apprentice program.
◆ Attend puppet rehearsals regularly for one year.
◆ Participate in ten performances, four of which must be away from the church.
◆ Participate in at least one puppet tour.

LEVEL THREE—ADVANCED PUPPETEER

◆ Complete journeyman program.
◆ Attend puppet rehearsals regularly for two years.
◆ Show progress in performance skills, including use of two rods, human-hand techniques, and live performance.
◆ Participate in at least two puppet tours.
◆ Successfully perform a lead role in one play or musical production.

LEVEL FOUR—MASTER PUPPETEER

◆ Complete advanced program.
◆ Attend puppet rehearsals regularly for three years.
◆ Be able to use at least three different "voices" in live performance.
◆ Write and perform a live puppet monologue or dialogue.
◆ Plan and direct one complete puppet rehearsal.

Award puppeteers different patches for each skill level. Encourage them to sew their patches to their puppetry shirts or jackets.

6. *Move to the puppet stage.* Have puppeteers work on positioning and on polishing their presentation. Go through the script several times, each time working out more details of movement and presentation.

7. *Add props, scenery, and costumes.* Practice with everything in place until each puppeteer feels comfortable with his or her part. Then you're ready to perform!

Steps one through four could be accomplished in your team's first exposure to the material, steps five and six during the second and third rehearsals, and step seven can wait until the fourth rehearsal.

Each group's learning rate will be different, so you'll need to adjust the learning schedule to fit your team. Experience will tell you what works best for your puppet team.

◆　◆　◆　◆　◆

Rehearsals are the foundation of your ministry with your team members. In rehearsals, not only do puppeteers learn their parts and develop their puppetry skills, they also interact with one another as members of a team. They learn to work through problems they have with other team members. And they discover the joy of "family" with other team members.

So make your team's rehearsals fun and meaningful. And provide ways for volunteers to grow through their relationships with one another.

CHAPTER 7

Write On!

J ohn's puppet team has been asked to do a program for the
local children's home. John's cousin is in this home, so he is
very excited about the opportunity to perform for the kids
there. John has shared his excitement about going, but the
director and the team don't have any scripts to fit the occasion.
John would like to write a puppet script for this performance, but
he has never written a puppet script before.

However...

John is great with puppets. His creativity shines every time
he picks one up. He and one of his best friends on the team
enjoy creating spontaneous conversations between their
puppet characters, and they often do ad-lib puppet announce-
ments in their Sunday School class, to the delight of all the
students in the class.

John and his best friend are perfect candidates for writing an
original puppet script.

◆　◆　◆　◆　◆

Sooner or later in puppet ministry, the time will come when you
can't find a suitable script for a specific need. Rather than miss an
opportunity for ministry, why not write your own skit or play?
Don't worry if you've never written anything before or if you don't
feel you're creative enough. All it takes is time, brainstorming, and
guidance.

Follow the simple steps outlined in this chapter, and soon you'll be writing scripts and plays for all occasions.

Finding Your Inspiration

John has decided to give scriptwriting a try. But where will he find ideas for topics, settings, and characters? What if he can't come up with any hot ideas?

◆   ◆   ◆   ◆   ◆

Some say there's no such thing as a new idea. In a way that's true, since our every thought is influenced by the billions of bits of information we've accumulated over the years.

So when you're looking for fresh ideas, don't feel bad about looking to various sources for inspiration. Although you should never use others' stories directly, you can draw from general concepts or ideas for use in a puppet drama. Creativity breeds creativity. So let others' creativity inspire your own ideas.

For starters, check out these resources:

Children's magazines and books—Visit a Christian bookstore and browse through the magazine and book titles. Look for hot topics or fads. You can also incorporate the latest sports stars, cartoon characters, and pop musicians into your puppet scripts.

TV shows—Some clever puppet scripts use familiar TV shows or formats to convey biblical truth. For example, build a script around a well-known talk show personality with fun guests. Be wise in your selection of a model from TV so that you don't offend your audience. Or rather than a particular title, you might simply adapt the *style* of a TV show—such as a family sitcom, a newscast, or even a special music TV countdown. Use your imagination for the host. For example, a camel puppet could host CMTV—Camel Music TV. He could supply all the latest news from Egypt and do a countdown of the popular songs of the children of Israel during the Exodus.

Small-group brainstorming—Get your puppet team to brainstorm ideas for puppet characters, musical pieces, and script topics your group would enjoy. After brainstorming, take the ideas and develop the ones that will adapt into a good script.

Bible stories—The Bible is filled with exciting stories that can make great puppet scripts. Outline the story details and make a list of all essential characters. Keep the story short and concise. For starters, adapt Jesus' parables or the story of David and Goliath.

◆　◆　◆　◆　◆

John considered these options and decided to concentrate on a Bible story that might relate to the kids in the children's home. He began by listing all the stories he knew that had kids in them. After talking to his director, John decided that he would write a story about the three Hebrew boys who were not living in their homes. He had also watched a fun children's video on this very same Bible story. He remembered some of the humor in that video, and it gave him an idea of his own. John decided to write a script about the three strongmen and their leader, Daniel.

Developing Your Style

Skits can take on several different styles. A skit conveying the power of God, for example, can be done with humor, serious narration, songs, or even no words at all. For each skit you produce, you must decide which style will most effectively get the message across.

The possibilities are endless. Consider these examples:
- serious—contemporary characters in real-life situations;
- fantasy—characters such as talking mushrooms, or unusual settings such as outer space or the ocean bottom;
- melodrama—hero and villain characters in an exaggerated style of good vs. evil;
- parable—characters acting out a parable from Scripture;
- time change—characters set in the past or in the future;
- multicultural—each character's appearance, conversation, and costume reflecting a specific cultural background such as a cowboy, a Hispanic, an Eskimo, or a Swede;
- TV or movie takeoff—story patterned after characters or format of a popular TV program or movie; and
- pantomime—characters acting out a story without words.

Style your skits to highlight the truths you want to convey. For example, a skit about materialism might work well in a TV game show format. Or a skit about communication might be interesting done as a pantomime. Use your imagination and try new ways to convey truths to your audience.

◆　◆　◆　◆　◆

After John talked with his puppet director, he decided to create a script about the three strongmen, patterned after a TV wrestling match. The first scene showed Daniel as trainer for the three strongmen. They were all asking for their favorite foods eaten back at home, but Daniel insisted on vegetables and lots of water. At first they complained to one another about Daniel, but when they saw their muscles growing, they began to smile and thank Daniel and God. In the second scene, the strongmen lifted weights and prepared for the fight by praying and promising to obey God no matter what happened.

Scene three was a complete surprise when their opponent showed up in the ring as a ninety-foot-tall statue they were expected to bow down to and worship. The three strongmen refused. The referee declared the statue the winner and ordered the three strongmen to be punished for losing this fight—by being thrown into a fiery furnace. However, the three not only remained strong in the fire but were doing a victory dance with a fourth figure in the flames...that of the likeness of the Son of God. When the strongmen were brought out, the trio did a victory chant.

Choosing Your Characters

John had decided to use strongmen as his three main characters, but he needed a personality for each of them. He thought about three well-known characters that kids might know and decided to use some of the characteristics of the three bears in the fairy tale. Shadrach became the biggest of the three, Meshach, the middle-sized boy, and Abednego, the smallest and often the whiner of the group, just like Baby Bear. But there's much more to character than just size, right?

◆　◆　◆　◆　◆

Right. Character development is crucial to a successful script. The most poignant message in the world will never reach the audience if the characters aren't believable.

The first question any scriptwriter must ask is "How many characters should I use?" The answer is always "As few as possible." Why? It's much easier to write and stage for one, two, or three characters than for larger numbers. And the more characters you have on stage at one time, the more difficult it is to have well-developed characters that interact well with one another.

Before you begin writing dialogue, write a character sketch for each character. Record his or her likes, dislikes, shortcomings, and other character traits. List expressions he or she would frequently use. Specify vocabulary and mannerisms that fit the character and make him or her stand out from all the others in the play. The better you define each character before you start writing, the easier the scriptwriting will be.

◆   ◆   ◆   ◆   ◆

John talked over his ideas with his director, and together they wrote a brief description for each character and listed several phrases or expressions that each might say in the various situations of the story. To limit the number of characters on stage at one time, they decided to replace Daniel with a narrator who told the story and introduced the three strongmen. John was well prepared when he sat down to actually write the dialogue.

Making a Scene

How many scenes will you need? In scripts shorter than three minutes, do everything in one scene. Let the dialogue or additional characters move the plot along instead of using several scenes or time settings to tell the story.

For longer scripts, determine the time frame of each scene, and keep action breaks short—but long enough for necessary backstage preparation. Few scripts should require more than three scenes to complete the action.

In longer skits, plan the two or three scenes so that each

character has a resting time, and puppeteers have a chance to rest their arms. Also don't have any one scene last more than five minutes. Otherwise the puppeteer's arm will tire, and the action will slow.

The first scene is vital. The opening needs to grab the audience's attention and get people involved emotionally. Keep action in mind. Have things *happening* on stage, rather than just having characters talk.

As you plan each scene, think about how the scene will look on stage. Write in the set changes and props you'll need to make the scene work. But keep your skits practical to perform. Your team may not have access to a potted palm tree to use in a Hawaiian skit, but chances are you can make a cardboard version to create the same effect.

Matching Your Audience

When creating a new skit, make sure the point you are trying to get across is within the mental grasp of your audience. For instance, does the vocabulary you're using fit the age level and background of your audience? It doesn't make sense to talk about political issues with small children or to discuss "life at home" with prison inmates. Also avoid using "Christianese"—terminology only longtime churchgoers would understand—unless you're doing it deliberately to make a point.

Have characters speak to the audience on its level. Never have a puppet talk down to an audience or speak over its head. One way to find out how your script comes across is to have individuals preview it and give you their opinions.

The audience's age helps you determine your puppet play's length. The following breakdown works well in deciding how long a play should be.

Age	Length
Grades one to three	five to six minutes
Grades four to six	seven to eight minutes
Junior high	ten to twelve minutes
High school and adults	up to fifteen minutes

Writing It Down

You know the concept for your play. You know the skit's style and purpose, and who your characters will be. Now all that remains is putting the finished work together and giving it a name.

The planning you've already done has probably taken several days. Use the "Script Planner" on page 66 to help you keep track of your ideas.

Your writing will reflect the quality of your preparation. By first considering the points already covered in this chapter, you should be able to write a complete, unified script in one sitting. Consider these pointers as you begin writing the dialogue:

- Include humor, but don't go overboard. Humor should highlight the message, not obstruct it.
- Repeat important ideas for emphasis.
- Use props and scenery to set the right mood.
- Keep puppets' lines short, emphasizing dialogue and minimizing long speeches.
- Create conflict or tension. Since most lessons in life are born out of conflict, include conflict in your script. Then draw your lesson from it. For example, two children wanting to play the same video game can create a conflict that leads to a lesson on sharing or servanthood.
- Stop when you've said enough. Don't prolong a script just to fill time or repeat a point after it has already been clearly made.
- Use adults to handle serious discussion following a play. Puppets are cartoonlike characters. Don't have them act overly serious or perform serious functions such as leading an altar call or praying with kids who want to become Christians.
- Don't depend only on dialogue to carry the message. Include actions that help carry the story.

◆　　◆　　◆　　◆　　◆

Practice writing a few simple scripts, and have friends and your puppeteers critique them. Then use their comments as you write

more complicated story lines. With practice, you'll soon be writing successful scripts for your puppet team to perform.

Script Planner

Title: _____

Intended audience: _____

Purpose: _____

Scriptures that confirm the skit's main idea:

Name of character   **Description of character**

1. _____ — _____
2. _____ — _____
3. _____ — _____
4. _____ — _____
5. _____ — _____
6. _____ — _____

Expressions or verbal mannerisms each character might use in conversation:

1.   4.

2.   5.

3.   6.

Style or format of skit:

Outline of each scene's action:

CHAPTER 8

All the World's a Stage

L ights! Camera! Action!"
    Martin has a habit of calling out that phrase during performances to cue his puppet team to begin a skit or song. That wouldn't be so odd, except his puppet team often performs in parks with no lights and no camera. In fact, the team often uses nothing more than a blanket for a stage. But Martin calls out anyway, "Lights! Camera! Action!"

Once each year, though, Martin's puppet team performs a full-length musical for the community, complete with lighting, sound, and, yes, even a video camera. And finally Martin's call makes sense.

◆　◆　◆　◆　◆

Puppet ministry can happen wherever people gather—whether that means an auditorium or a parking lot. Having a nice stage—complete with lighting and sound—can make a puppet team's performance really shine. But doing a skit from behind a dumpster for a group of neighborhood kids can have the same lasting effects on people's lives.

So just what does having a nice stage set accomplish? Sets enhance your program's message. Nothing more, nothing less. Your puppet team is not crippled if you don't have a nice set. And neither has your team "arrived" just because you do have one.

So design your sets to enhance the puppet team's message, but don't depend on your set to carry the message alone.

Stage Matters

A puppet stage gives puppeteers something to hide behind and spotlights the puppets themselves. With that broad purpose, a puppet stage can be anything from a simple sheet to a multilevel, multicurtain stage designed for grand puppet productions. Choose your team's stage (or stages) based on the number of puppets you use and your audience's needs.

Let's look at possible stage ideas you can use as your puppet team performs and grows.

The refrigerator box stage—In certain cases, you can use a refrigerator or freezer box as a stage. Just lay the box on its side and cut a slit along the top for the puppets to appear through. Because of space limitations, use this type of stage with only one or two puppeteers.

If needed, you can break down the box and carry it to different locations. This type of stage might be ideal for backyard Bible clubs or in situations where a few puppeteers are traveling short distances and doing multiple performances. Since it's made of cardboard, however, this type of stage won't last for more than a few performances.

The microphone stand stage—To create this stage, connect each end of a 6-foot 1x4-inch board to an adjustable microphone stand. You can do this by attaching two metal flanges and two 6-inch lengths of plastic or metal pipe to the board's flat side. This allows the board to sit on the tops of the stands, held in place by the pipes. Use Velcro to hang a curtain along the length of the board. See page 69.

Because you can adjust the stage height easily, this stage type works well for puppet teams with volunteers of various heights and sizes.

The improvised stage—Occasionally you may find yourself in a situation where you don't have a real stage to work with. If that happens, just use whatever's available. Items such as a pulpit, a piano, a room divider, a chalkboard, a table turned on its side, or a blanket held up between two people can all be used as stages in a pinch.

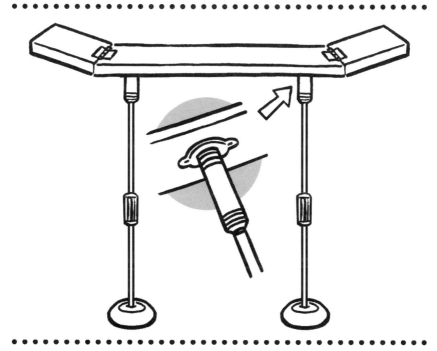

The connected panel stage—This stage is made from three to five panels joined together with hinges. For the panels, use plywood or a wooden framework covered with canvas or fabric. This stage sets up easily but requires a large vehicle for travel. For best results, design the stage so it will fold flat for travel and storage. See page 70.

The plastic pipe stage—The plastic pipe stage is commonly used by most beginner puppet teams. PVC plastic plumbing pipe is universally available and inexpensive. The $1^1/2$-inch-diameter white pipe is recommended and is available at plumbing supply or home improvement stores. The pipe generally comes in 10-foot lengths, but it can easily be cut with a hacksaw.

The pipes can be connected to create a two-level performance stage with a backdrop. See the "Two-Level Stage With Backdrop" schematic on page 71. This stage schematic can also be easily adapted to a single-level stage.

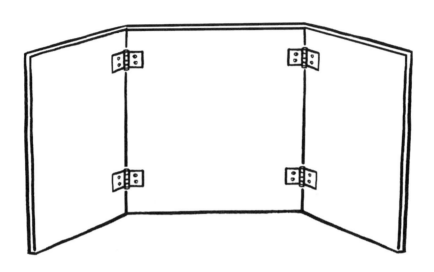

Set the top of the front level at about 48 to 52 inches off the floor, which allows puppeteers to perform in a kneeling position. Set the top of the second level at about 5 feet 8 inches to 6 feet off the floor. This allows a second group of puppeteers to work from a standing position. Also allow 2 feet of stage width for each puppeteer. For example, if you plan to have three puppeteers on stage at one time, you'll need a stage at least 6 feet wide. Once you know your puppet team's performance needs, you can easily design your own puppet stage using PVC pipe and connectors.

Use a velour, crushed velvet, or heavy polyester fabric to form a curtain. Simply sew a casing at one edge of the material so you can insert the pipe through the material. Then slip the curtains over the pipes and assemble the pipes to form the stage. See the illustration on page 72.

Once the curtain is in place, use Velcro spots and strips to hold the curtain panels together so no gaps or poorly fitted joints exist.

To hold the plastic-pipe framework together, either use duct tape to connect the joints or drill holes through the joints and use nails or bolts to secure them together.

Two-Level Stage With Backdrop

Many puppet teams find this stage is the most versatile and least cumbersome to travel with. When fully assembled, the stage can hold up to ten puppeteers. It also works well for smaller productions that involve frequent scene changes. While puppeteers perform one scene on the lower stage, another group of puppeteers can be preparing for the next scene on the upper stage.

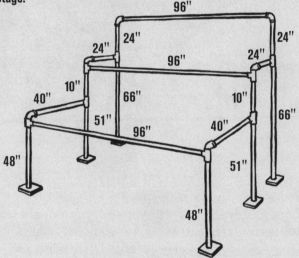

Here's a list of the materials you will need to build this stage:

◆ eight 10-foot lengths of 1¹/₂-inch plastic pipe
◆ two 90-degree ells
◆ four 90-degree street ells
◆ eight tees
◆ six 1¹/₂-inch male adapters
◆ six 1¹/₂-inch cast-iron floor flanges
◆ six wood bases, each 10×10×1 inches

You may have to adjust the pipe lengths slightly to make the stage appear level. That's because pipe connectors vary slightly in length and shape, and they can cause the joints to fit differently.

The aluminum tripod stage—In recent years a new technology in puppet stages has become widely preferred. Aluminum tripod stages are made from lightweight, adjustable, telescoping crossbars and tripods adapted from their original use as photography background stands.

An aluminum tripod stage makes setup and takedown easy, and it's lighter to travel with. The stage offers height and width adjustability, adaptability to multi-level platforms, and the flexibility to configure the stage in many different ways. Although the cost is significantly higher than PVC pipe, the many benefits of the aluminum tripod stage have made it the "stage of choice" for veteran puppet ministry directors. See the diagram on page 73 for a basic aluminum tripod stage.

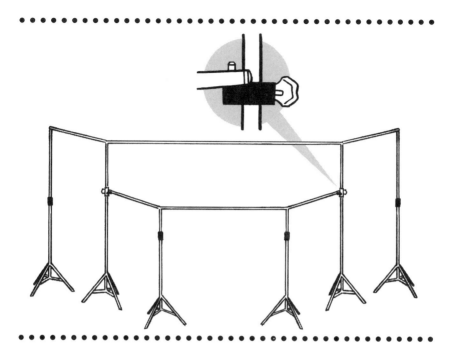

Props and Prop Racks

Props are often used to help convey the message of a puppet song or skit. Props can be objects, like a toy saxophone or plastic guitar, or they can be hand-made signs depicting objects or words to help the audience understand and enjoy the song or skit. For example, if the words of a puppet song say "Moses parted the Red Sea with his rod," a creative puppet team director might have a puppeteer's gloved hand come up holding a rod and then part two foam core "waves" with that rod. Or if the song gives three steps to salvation, three prop signs might present the words: "Turn away from sin," "Tell God you're sorry!" and "Receive Jesus."

Props are often used throughout a song or skit to help "set the stage," so they are left in place for the entire presentation. In this case, prop racks are used to support the prop in its place. For example, if you were doing a song about Noah's ark, you might want an "ark" prop to be in place for the entire song. The ark could be supported by a prop rack rather than by a puppeteer holding it for a long period of time. The prop rack is a long piece of wood connected to the vertical side supports of the stage. Using metal U-bolts, the prop rack can be attached and secured and will support the weight of a cardboard or foam core prop. See diagram below.

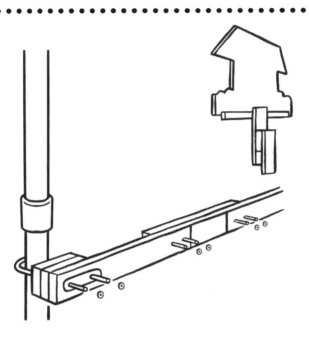

Prop tables are also easy to use inside the stage to support such prop items as a drum set, keyboard, computer, or lamp. A prop table consists of a piece of plywood attached to a microphone stand with a metal flange. Often the wood is painted black or covered with fabric to blend in with the stage curtains. The adjustability of the microphone stand allows you to set the height of the prop table at your desired level. See diagram on page 75.

Sound Advice

When you begin a puppet ministry, your team's attention and energies usually go into acquiring attractive puppets and mastering basic manipulation techniques. Your only sound equipment may be a portable stereo for amplifying recorded songs and skits.

If you perform primarily in a church sanctuary or a children's church auditorium, you will probably be able to utilize existing sound equipment. If you do any "live voice" performing, you will want to invest in one or more headset microphones to allow the puppeteer(s) freedom of movement.

As the ministry of your team expands, and as you travel more, you'll want to invest in a more powerful portable sound system to enhance your performances.

Sound systems come in all sizes, but one-piece, portable, high output systems usually work best for puppet teams. Several manufacturers make lightweight, compact, and powerful sound systems with speakers, amplifier, and mixer all in one small suit-case-sized case. This type of system works well for puppet teams because it's portable and easy to set up. Most models allow you to plug one or more microphones directly into them and also connect a line directly from your recorded-sound source.

These portable sound systems can be purchased at most

electronic shops that carry sound equipment or from companies that specialize in equipment for puppet ministry teams.

Beautiful Scenery

Scenery helps set the mood for your presentation. In puppetry, scenery can be draped over the stage curtain or the backdrop curtain, or made to stand alone next to the stage.

You can make scenery out of just about anything. If you'll need a piece of scenery only once, simple cardboard or construction paper may suffice. If you want more permanent scenery, here are four resources you can use:

Foam core—These white sheets are made from two thin cardboard pieces with a foam core between. Foam core cuts easily and works well for free-standing props, scenery panels, or backdrops. You can purchase it in sheets as large as 4x8 feet.

Polyurethane foam sheets—Polyurethane foam sheets can be rolled up like carpet, which makes this scenery product excellent for groups that travel long distances. The sheets come in various thicknesses, but generally the 3/8-inch thickness works best. You can paint right on the foam with spray paint or acrylic paint. You can also use permanent markers to highlight or outline.

The foam sheets attach easily to stage curtains with Velcro. Glue a wide strip of belting material across the top of the foam panel, then sew the Velcro patches to the strip. That way you avoid tearing the foam.

Cotton "duck" fabric—This material works well when you want to paint your scenery right onto the stage curtain. Tempera and acrylic paints both work, and a marker can be used to add final touches. Before you paint, however, attach the material to a plywood sheet, and lay it flat so the material won't wrinkle and the paint won't run.

Projected scenery—The easiest type of scenery to travel with, and the quickest to change, is projected scenery from an overhead projector or from a laptop computer and video projector. Projected scenery requires a rear screen setup located behind the puppet action. It is necessary to have sufficient staging space behind your puppet stage to allow for enough distance to clearly project the image. You may also need a projection table with adjustable height to allow your image to be cast on a screen above the puppeteers' heads. Although rear projection screens can be expensive, you can make your own using a wood or plastic-pipe frame and a screen made from white sheets or a white plastic shower curtain stretched tightly across the frame.

Brilliant Lighting

You may be asked to perform in areas so poorly lit that your puppets become shadows on the stage. Or you may find a script you like that requires special lighting, such as a night scene or a storm. When that happens, you may want to consider building or purchasing a lighting system.

A low-budget lighting system can be constructed by building light towers from plastic pipe and using hardware store "clamp-on" lights attached to the plastic-pipe light bars. A more expensive option is to purchase aluminum or steel light trees and attach Par 38 light cans to them. If you aren't familiar with wiring and lighting, you should find someone in your church or community who can assist you in the design, safety, control, and portability factors you desire for your lighting system.

Theatrical supply houses and companies that supply equipment to traveling groups offer several levels of lighting systems. These systems consist of a lighting control board, tripod lighting stands, several Par 38 light cans and bulbs, colored gels, and extension cords. The slightly more advanced systems include dimmer packs that allow you to use fewer extension cords for easier setup.

Whatever lighting system you use, arrange the lights carefully around the stage area. Place the lights high enough on the stage's periphery so all shadows cast by the puppets fall inside the stage, unseen by the audience. Locate the lighting poles to the sides so they don't obstruct the audience's view.

Other Special Lighting

You can use lighting to achieve a variety of special effects. Turn on to these special light sources:

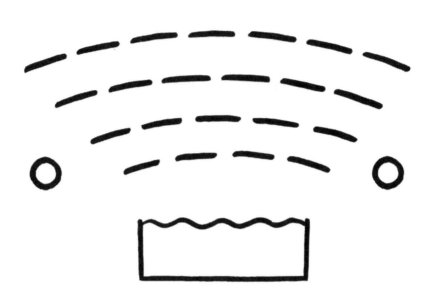

Black light—There are three basic ingredients needed for black light puppetry: black lights, fluorescent materials, and a darkened performance area. Black light makes fluorescent puppets and props glow in a powerful and exciting way. The bright color of such items moving through the darkness provides special impact and focuses the attention of the audience on only those things that show up against the darkness. Because only the fluorescent puppets and props can be seen, a puppeteer can actually stand up in the stage or perform in front of the black curtains of the stage while holding puppets or props in any position. Black gloves, shirts, hoods, and other black clothing hide the puppeteer from view while the fluorescent items glow clearly. It is important to position the black light ten to twelve inches away from the puppet or prop to be illuminated. To accomplish this, black lights are typically hung just inside the top level of the puppet stage or, for performing in front of the stage, placed on the floor at the front. Many teams apply this technique to simply using white gloves and signing the words for songs in black light.

Strobe lights—Strobe lights flash brilliantly at regular intervals. They can be used to depict lightning, stop-action effects, or disco-style lighting.

Spotlights—Spotlights may be rented or purchased from a theatrical supply house. Or you can make your own. One inexpensive way to achieve a spotlight effect is to cut a hole in a slide-size piece of cardboard and insert it in a slide projector. Create several cardboard slides with different-sized holes and various patterns.

Mirror balls—Create your own mirror ball by cementing small mirror tiles to a plastic-foam ball. When a spotlight or other concentrated light source hits the ball, you get a "starry night" effect throughout the room.

One Step at a Time

Some veteran puppet teams collect impressive arrays of equipment, such as individual headset microphones, walkie-talkies, lighting standards, individually controlled spotlights and black lights, rear projection screens, and large, impressive sets with changeable scenery.

Operations of this size obviously entail a great deal of planning and expense, and at times these ministries might discourage a beginning puppet team.

Be assured that special equipment isn't necessary to have an effective ministry. Do the best possible job of ministry with the tools and resources you have. Never purchase "advanced" equipment simply to impress an audience or to be better than another team. If you do purchase advanced technical equipment—such as a lighting or sound system—make sure your motivation is to clarify the message you're presenting and to highlight your puppeteers' skills.

Anyone can put together a slick production. But what matters is that the heart of your message gets across to your audience.

CHAPTER 9

Using Puppets in Outreach Ministry

Christy Watkins' puppet team was quickly a big hit in her local church. She had many young people wanting to join the team, audiences were really enjoying the team's performances at church, and she felt a sense of spiritual satisfaction that God had truly led her into a very special ministry.

But after the many rehearsals, extensive prop building, and fine-tuning of her team's productions, it became clear that her team needed to perform at other places beyond the local church. Doors started opening at other churches, Christian schools, public schools, summer camps, inner-city ministries, and even national and international conferences.

The true story of the P.O.W.E.R. Company provides a great model for building an outreach puppet ministry. Begin by performing in your own church and building a quality performance repertoire. Establish an atmosphere of fellowship and community among the team leaders and puppeteers. Encourage prayer, volunteering, and financial support from the church body.

Second, make your ministry available in the community for performances at nursing homes, day-care centers, schools, parks, civic organizations, celebrations, fairs, and other opportunities. By making your team available to all interested parties, you will discover that your team's ministry and unity will prosper as you follow God's leading.

Third, seriously consider taking your team on an extended ministry tour, performing a set program each night in churches, schools, parks, and other venues open to you. There are many reasons a tour can enhance your team ministry and long-term success:

- Taking your performance to new places gives your team members an added incentive to perfect the details that separate a mediocre performance from an outstanding one.
- A puppet ministry tour provides a great opportunity for spiritual growth. Puppeteers learn to minister to others through their performances and through daily encounters with other team members.
- Many young people never have the opportunity to travel, and a puppet tour becomes the highlight of their year.
- Puppet tours provide great publicity in your home church and encourage potential members to become a part of the church and the puppet ministry.

Setting Up a Tour

The most crucial time of any tour is the time *before* you leave. Tours that aren't planned well are like time bombs waiting to explode. Take the time and energy to set up a detailed tour—including travel route, sleeping arrangements, and menus for each day—and your tour will have much less chance of problems.

Determining an itinerary—Before you do any planning, decide on a destination. You can do this effectively by asking your team members where their Christian relatives live. Also check your own family line. Good ol' Aunt Louisa, whom you haven't seen in years, just might be more than happy to host your puppet ministry at her church.

Also look for locations that offer attractions for young people, such as amusement parks or museums. See if you know anyone in that area, such as a minister in a sister church or a one-time church member who has now moved away.

Another option for choosing a destination is to find a church that really *needs* a children's ministry—such as a summer Bible school or backyard Bible clubs.

Remember to listen to your team members too. One leader took his volunteers on a trip to Nashville, only to find that none of them were country music fans or big on shopping. The leaders in the group had decided it would be fun, and it was—but not for the rest of the team. Ask your volunteers what they'd like to do while they're on the road. And plan your route accordingly.

Wherever you decide to go, be sure you have a contact person on the other end—someone who'll be responsible for housing, setup, and promotion. If you have set up multiple performances in different towns, secure a contact person in each town. You need someone to be your eyes and ears in each location.

After you've decided on a destination, determine the number of travel days you have available, and set an agenda for each day—places you'll visit, sights you'll see, and where you'll perform or lodge that evening. Keep your average under 250 miles per day, especially if you're traveling several days in a row.

If you're lodging in a city where you're not performing, call a minister in the area and ask about housing possibilities. Many churches have gymnasiums where groups can sleep. Or churches may volunteer to house you in their homes even if you don't perform in their church. If neither of those options work, ask the minister to recommend a local hotel.

Planning a tour budget—With proper planning, a tour doesn't have to cost much. When you schedule a performance at a church, ask for four things:

1. Supper and breakfast;
2. Lodging in homes;
3. An offering; and
4. A sincere effort to promote good attendance.

If you can schedule a performance most days of the tour, much of your cost will come from lunches and the fuel for your vehicle. Most tour groups set aside one or two days for fun and sightseeing, too. Offerings will help cover all these expenses.

Even if you have to buy all three meals, you can still find creative ways to cut costs. For example, go to a grocery store, buy picnic supplies, and eat in a park; or ask host families to fix sack lunches for the following day.

When budgeting your trip's cost, estimate high on your expenditures, estimate low on the offerings you'll receive, and charge each puppeteer enough so you'll have money left over to keep your team financially afloat.

Communicating the facts—Mail an information packet with the following items to each church you're planning to perform in:
- a cover letter explaining the tour theme;
- a description of the performance;
- promotional fliers and posters, including a picture and description of your team;
- clarification of what you require from the host church (offering, lodging, and meals); and
- a step-by-step explanation of what the contact person must do to prepare for your team's arrival.

Send these packets four to eight weeks before the tour dates.

Communicate with your contact people by telephone to clarify the arrangements. Then mail a second information packet that further clarifies what you're requesting the host church to supply. Also send the contact person a list of the people in your group—including their ages and gender—so the contact person can arrange housing for your puppeteers. Also include information regarding arrival and departure times, so the puppeteers' hosts will know when to pick the volunteers up and when to bring them back to the church the morning after the performance.

Informing the parents—Schedule a meeting before the tour to clarify what you expect from each team member. Include your policies regarding
- amount of spending money needed;
- guidelines for behavior in host homes and churches;
- guidelines for travel in the van or car;
- expectations regarding relationships between guys and girls;
- type of clothing needed;
- amount of luggage allowed;
- whether you'll allow personal stereos or other electronic devices; and
- expectations and responsibilities of volunteers or chaperones.

Provide volunteers with logistical information such as departure and return times and a list of items they will need to pack. Also consult local medical and insurance agencies to know what forms and precautions are needed to protect against any injuries that might occur. If you have minors in your group of puppeteers, make parents and kids aware of any legal issues that concern them.

Preparing the troops—Schedule one or two final dress rehearsals before you leave—to make sure you have all the "bugs" worked out of your program. In fact, consider scheduling a "trial run" performance close to home to help your puppeteers build their confidence.

Hitting the road—Consider these tips as you prepare to leave:

- Don't wait until the last minute to pack your vehicle or trailer. Pack it ahead of time to make sure everything fits.
- Make sure your scenery and props are cushioned so they won't be damaged in transit.
- Get *exact* directions to each sponsor church on your route.

Working as a Team

Prior to the trip, assign every team member a specific responsibility for setup and takedown. Responsibilities include: stage setup, sound and lights setup, puppet preparation, ushering, cleanup, and packing the van or trailer after a performance.

Allow time for group prayer before your performance to give volunteers a chance to express their concerns and requests to God. And seek God's working through your performance. Include your church's host and contact person in this time. Also use this time to encourage team members. Tell them you believe in them and in their ability to minister as God works through them. Your support goes a long way in helping volunteers strive to do their best.

Making Memories

Your puppet tour should be a *fun* time. Between your performances, schedule fun activities together, such as visiting an amusement park or a water park. Or take your team bowling, canoeing, sightseeing, or even shopping at a local mall.

Assign one of the volunteers to be the tour photographer. Have him or her take lots of pictures of the puppet team at work and at play. Have a "picture party" when you get home, and invite prospective puppeteers to join you.

You can also start a few tour traditions. For instance, when your team takes the stage down after each performance, use the discarded duct tape to create a tape ball. Add to the ball after each performance. Then, at the end of the tour, present the tape ball to the team member who best exhibited a servant attitude.

Many puppet teams sponsor "coming home" celebrations when the team returns home from a puppet tour. The team performs its puppet presentation for the home congregation. Then puppeteers share testimonies and memories of the trip with church members. Many teams present a slide show of the tour. Finally, the church members and puppeteers celebrate together with games and a refreshment time.

Think up your own tradition ideas and use them to make your puppet ministry tour even more special.

Creating Spiritual Impact

Plan meaningful spiritual times for team members while on a puppet tour. Try these suggestions:

◆ Schedule a "quiet time" each day when puppeteers can get by themselves and read the Bible, write in a journal, or pray. Provide devotional materials for them to use during this time.

◆ Have team members take turns leading devotions during the tour. Schedule group devotions when people are alert—not right before they go to bed.

◆ Assign each person a "secret pal" or "secret agent." Challenge team members to make small gifts, share encouraging Bible verses, or write special notes to their special person during the tour.

◆ Schedule a final sharing time near the end of the tour, and allow everyone to share concerns and blessings. Then pray together and have secret pals reveal themselves.

Puppet tours can be great fun and a great way to encourage team members' spiritual growth. Let guidelines in this chapter inspire you to take your puppeteers on an adventure in ministry. You'll be amazed at the ways your volunteers grow in their faith and relationships. And you'll be thankful for the way your puppet ministry touches lives.

CHAPTER 10

Avoiding the Puppet Cemetery

Many churches start puppet ministries with great enthusiasm and purpose, only to have them die within six months or a year. To prevent your puppet team's premature demise, let's take a trip to "Puppet Garden Cemetery" and read the epitaphs on tombstones of failed puppet ministries. Perhaps you can avoid the pitfalls that have ended the ministries of others.

Cemetery Tour

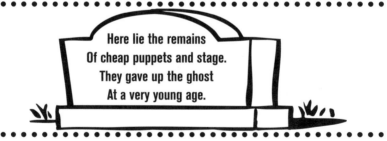

Here lie the remains
Of cheap puppets and stage.
They gave up the ghost
At a very young age.

Whether you purchase ready-made puppets and stages or make your own, invest your money and energy into resources that will last. Don't plan to just "get by," but plan from the beginning for a ministry that will last many years. Look at the big picture, not just at your first performance.

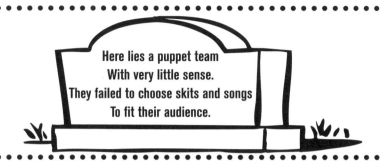

Here lies a puppet team
With very little sense.
They failed to choose skits and songs
To fit their audience.

Keep your team's repertoire broad. You can't perform the same material for a teenage group that you would for a preschool children's church. Likewise, a performance at a pastor's convention demands a different thrust than a ministry at an inner-city mission. Audiences range greatly in age, interests and background, and the material you choose for a specific audience should match the needs of that audience.

Here lie some puppeteers
Who were dead all along.
Their skills were all self-taught,
And all of them were wrong.

Make sure you learn correct puppetry techniques and skills from the beginning. It's difficult to unlearn bad habits. Puppet ministry has a bad reputation in many churches because of poor techniques and skills. With proper training, excellence will become your team's trademark.

Use these suggestions for learning correct techniques:
- Attend puppetry training seminars.
- Rent videotapes of proper puppetry techniques.
- Visit rehearsals of established puppet teams.
- Observe other puppeteers closely on televised puppet shows.

- Enter competitions where you'll be evaluated.
- Have team members evaluate one another.

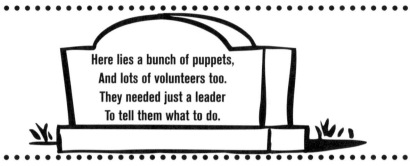

Here lies a bunch of puppets,
And lots of volunteers too.
They needed just a leader
To tell them what to do.

A puppet ministry leader needs to learn basic puppetry skills to begin training others. Leaders who decide to "wing it" generally find that their puppeteers lose interest because they don't feel what they're doing is excellent or worthwhile.

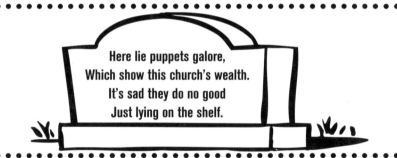

Here lie puppets galore,
Which show this church's wealth.
It's sad they do no good
Just lying on the shelf.

To maintain interest, a puppet team must remain active and perform regularly. Puppeteers lose interest quickly if all they do is practice. Performing before a live audience provides the positive feedback volunteers need to develop purpose and excitement.

Here lies a puppet team,
Masters at what they do.
But no one comes to watch them;
They never do anything new.

Many puppet ministries die from sheer boredom. Any puppet skit or song can become boring to the puppet team and to audiences after too much repetition. To maintain excitement and anticipation in rehearsals and performances, continually introduce new material to challenge team members.

Here lie the "might've beens,"
Who never had puppetry chances.
They just sat back and complained
Because they lacked finances.

Although some established puppet teams have many puppets, elaborate stages, sound equipment, lighting equipment, matching shirts, and possibly even a van or bus to travel in, these items certainly aren't essential to a group's ministry efforts.

All you need to begin with is a puppet or two, a helper or two, something to hide behind, and a calling from God to minister. Lack of finances shouldn't be a major problem. Start where you are—with what you have. Do the best you can, and trust God to help you in your areas of need.

Here lies an entertaining team
That loved to tell a joke.
But fun alone without sharing Christ
Has caused this team to croak!

Although puppets can be entertaining, your team needs to present more than just fun and games. In fact, most of the plays, skits, and songs you spend time on should be chosen for the biblical message they convey.

Puppetry can be a powerful tool, and what puppets do and say will leave a lasting impression on audiences and puppeteers. Don't waste your group's efforts or opportunities—work together to gain eternal results.

An Ongoing Ministry

The puppet cemetery shows you pitfalls to avoid as your puppet ministry grows. But even avoiding those grave markers won't guarantee success. You need to take positive steps to keep your puppet ministry alive and thriving.

The secret to an ongoing puppet ministry is to motivate team members to take ownership of the ministry and do the best they can with the talents they have. Read these suggestions on how to motivate yourself and your team members to do the best for God.

Earn respect. No puppet team will get far without firm, directive leadership. You must earn your puppet team's respect, both as a puppeteer and as a spiritual leader. Strive to be excellent at what you do. Let puppeteers join with you in directing the ministry, but don't allow them to control you. Volunteers need you to be a solid leader so they can explore their own leadership abilities under your guidance.

Use positive reinforcement. Avoid criticism and putdowns. Find something to praise in each team member's performance. Give puppeteers small awards and verbal praise for projects they accomplish successfully. Avoid giving demerits or embarrassing team members in any way.

Perform often. When your team fails to perform regularly, their skills grow dull—along with their motivation to keep working. Scheduled performances give volunteers goals to work toward.

Keep things classy. A catchy team name and logo, and a flashy business card or brochure, will send team spirit soaring. Matching T-shirts for puppeteers are great if you can afford them. Let volunteers know that what they're doing is important and deserves recognition.

Encourage openness and creativity. Ask your puppeteers for their suggestions for ways to improve as a team. You may not be able to use all their ideas, but giving team members a chance to express their opinions affirms their importance. If your team members seem hesitant to discuss their opinions openly, have them respond to questionnaires you design. Or set up a suggestion box in the rehearsal room.

Encourage long-term commitment. Consider giving awards to volunteers who have stayed on the team for three years or longer. You might have a "Three Years of Service" plaque made for these people, or similar plaques to celebrate and reward those volunteers who have given years of faithful service to this ministry.

♦ ♦ ♦ ♦ ♦

Puppet ministry provides unique opportunities to minister to hurting people. A puppet isn't threatening. It can open avenues of communication that real people can't. In ways we cannot always understand, puppets speak to the child in each of us and help us bring our hurts to the surface for comfort and healing.

A puppet team did a program for a group of developmentally disabled adults. As the show progressed, the puppeteers were amazed at how the adults opened up to the puppets, treating them almost like new friends.

One adult, Larry, always looked at the ground because he was shy. But when the puppets appeared on stage, he couldn't resist peeking. The puppeteers noticed Larry's curiosity and encouraged him to try a puppet himself. He did.

Eventually, Larry's shy puppet eased onto the stage. Although the puppet never said a word, the puppeteers were deeply moved to see the big smile on Larry's face.

That's puppet ministry. People reaching people through fantasy and fun. Puppets will open doors for ministry that you never thought possible. And with proper guidance and motivation, your puppet ministry will keep growing for many years to come.

CHAPTER 11

Puppet Scripts

Puppets depend on humor to catch the attention of their listeners. However, once they gain the attention of an audience, puppets can be powerful tools to drive home the truth found in God's Word. Use these scripts to reach audiences of all ages with God's love.

Where's the Fire?

by Todd Liebenow

SCRIPTURE REFERENCE:

Exodus 3:1-10

• •

MOSES: (*Scurrying around packing for his trip back to Egypt*) Now let me see, where did I put my favorite sandals?

FIREMAN: (*Enters.*) Excuse me, sir.

MOSES: Oh my goodness, you scared me!

FIREMAN: I need to talk to you for a moment, sir.

MOSES: This really isn't a good time for me. I'm getting ready for a long trip.

FIREMAN: This won't take but a moment, sir. I'm from the fire department. We've had reports of a forest fire in the area near here. So we're just asking the locals to move out for a while. Go visit some relatives or something. You know, get out of the way so we can do our job. You understand, don't you, sir?

MOSES: A forest fire? But we're in the middle of the desert.

FIREMAN: Well OK, it's not a "forest fire." It's just a burning bush, but to us in the desert, it's a forest fire. When you don't have much vegetation to start with, you kind of want to protect what you've got. Don't you think so, sir?

MOSES: I suppose. But you really have no reason to be concerned about that burning bush.

FIREMAN: Is that so? (*Pauses in frustration.*) What's your name, sir?

MOSES: Uh, Moses.

FIREMAN: Moses, huh. Tell me, Mr. Moses, just what do you do for a living?

MOSES: Well, I'm a shepherd.

FIREMAN: I see, a shepherd. And I suppose you feel that your experience in the area of sheepherding somehow gives you some sort of special knowledge about fire safety that a trained fire protection professional like myself couldn't possibly know.

MOSES: That's not what I meant—

FIREMAN: Look, buddy, I come from a long line of firefighters. My father was a firefighter, and so was his father, and so was—

MOSES: All I was trying to say is that I've seen this burning bush, and believe me, it won't cause any harm.

FIREMAN: You saw this burning bush?

MOSES: Yes, I was watching my father-in-law's sheep when I came across it.

FIREMAN: Did you see any kids playing with torches in the area?

MOSES: The fire wasn't started by any person.

FIREMAN: I wouldn't rule out arson so quickly if I were you, Mr. Moses.

MOSES: The fire was fire from heaven.

FIREMAN: Fire from heaven! Umm...like a Sodom and Gomorrah type of thing here?

MOSES: No, nothing like that. The bush was on fire, but it didn't burn up. Somehow God was in the flames of that burning bush. And he spoke to me.

FIREMAN: The bush spoke to you?

MOSES: Not the bush. It was God. He called me by name and told me to take off my shoes because I was standing on holy ground.

FIREMAN: Slow down, sir! I'm still trying to figure out that part about the bush talking to you.

MOSES: The Lord told me that he had heard the cries of his people held captive in Egypt, and that the time had come for them to be freed. He said that I would be the one to lead them out of Egypt.

FIREMAN: You?

MOSES: I didn't believe him at first, either. I never considered myself to be a very good speaker. I didn't know how I would be able to convince Pharaoh to release God's people. To be honest with you, I'm still a little unsure about it. But God showed me how he could help me to do amazing miracles to try and convince Pharaoh to listen.

FIREMAN: What sort of miracles?

MOSES: Well, God told me to put my staff on the ground, and when I did, it changed into a snake. Then when I picked up the snake, it turned back into my staff.

FIREMAN: Sounds like too much smoke inhalation to me, sir. People have been known to hallucinate when around fire and smoke for too long.

MOSES: It wasn't a hallucination. It was the power of God.

FIREMAN: Yeah, yeah, yeah. So, is that the trip you're getting ready for? You're heading off to Egypt?

MOSES: Heading to Egypt to free God's people! God told me that my brother Aaron was already on the way to meet me there. He will help me speak to Pharaoh.

FIREMAN: Is he a pyromaniac too?

MOSES: Look, I didn't set the bush on fire. God was speaking through that bush.

FIREMAN: Well, I hope your trip goes well and all. But you sound like trouble to me, Mr. Moses, if that is your real name. I'm gonna keep an eye on you. I mean, you shouldn't just go around talking to burning bushes. Didn't anyone ever tell you not to play with fire?

MOSES: What can I say? When God talks, I listen.

FIREMAN: All right, go on and get ready for your trip. But I don't want to catch you someday out in the middle of the desert with a big pillar of fire or something like that, got it?

MOSES: You never know what might happen.

(*Both exit.*)

• •

Name That Commandment!

by Liz VonSeggen

SCRIPTURE REFERENCES:

Exodus 20:1-17; Mark 12:29-31

MC: It's time to play *Name That Commandment!* Our first contestant today comes all the way from Oklahoma City, Oklahoma. His name is Ollie Wright. Please welcome Ollie!

OLLIE: (*Enters.*) Oh, I'm so nervous. I've never been on TV, you know.

MC: Our second contestant today is Winnie Hope from Chicago, Illinois. Let's welcome to the show Miss Winnie Hope!

WINNIE: (*Enters.*) Oh, I'm so excited to be here. I just hope I can win, win, win!

MC: You both know how the game is played. When you know the answer, push your buzzer and if you're right, we'll put $500 on your scoreboard. If you're wrong, your opponent will get the chance to answer the question and double that amount. Ready? (*They nod.*) Question number one: What is the first commandment from God?

WINNIE: (*Buzzes.*) The first commandment? That's easy. Be number one. Put yourself first.

MC: Oh, I'm sorry, Winnie. That is not the correct answer. Ollie, do you know God's first commandment?

OLLIE: Ah ... let's see. I think the first and most important commandment is "Love the Lord your God with all your heart and with all your soul and with all your mind and with all your strength."

MC: Well, that is a very important command, but my answer card says, "You shall have no other gods before me." I'm sorry, neither one of you scored on

that question. Question number two: What is the
commandment most often quoted by your mother?

OLLIE: (*Buzzes first.*) Always tell the truth.

WINNIE: (*Buzzes also.*) Don't steal the cookies!

MC: Well, you both have the right idea. "You shall not give
false testimony" and "You shall not steal" are both
commandments. We will give each of you $500 for
your answers this round. *My* mom always told me,
"Honor your father and your mother." That's
commandment number five!

WINNIE: I'm just sure I can get the next one. I'm ready!

MC: All right. Let's see who our winner will be. Question
number three: What is the shortest commandment?

WINNIE: (*Buzzes first.*) I know. I know. "Jesus wept"!

MC: Shortest commandment, not shortest verse. Ollie, do
you know?

OLLIE: I think it is "You shall not kill."

MC: That's right! You just earned $1,000, making your total
$1,500.

WINNIE: Oh no! Look at your score! You're killing me . . . and
didn't you just say that God commanded, "You shall
not kill"?

MC: God was talking about murder, not losing a quiz game.
We have one final question for both of you. Take your
time and think! Question number four: What is the
greatest commandment of them all?

OLLIE: (*Buzzes.*) I think I know the answer, but I'm a little
confused.

MC: Please just answer the question.

OLLIE: When he was asked that very same question, Jesus said
that the greatest commandment was this: "Love the
Lord your God with all your heart and with all your
soul and with all your mind and with all your
strength."

WINNIE: Isn't that the same answer you gave for commandment number one?

OLLIE: Right! That is exactly why I'm confused. You see, I thought when you asked for commandment number one, you meant which is the greatest commandment, and I remembered what Jesus said.

MC: Wow! Your answer for question number four is correct, but let me confer with the judges to see what they decide regarding our very first question. (*Exits.*)

WINNIE: Good luck, Ollie. I sure wish I knew as much about God's commandments as you do.

OLLIE: You can, you know, and I'd be glad to teach you. That's the least I could do.

WINNIE: Why would you do that for me?

OLLIE: Well, because the second greatest commandment tells me to.

WINNIE: No way! You're saying God made a commandment that says, "You shall help Winnie learn my commandments"?

OLLIE: Not exactly. The second greatest commandment Jesus said is "Love your neighbor as you love yourself."

MC: (*Enters.*) Good news, Ollie and Winnie! The judges say Ollie was right on both questions, because I did not make it clear whether I wanted God's first commandment given to Moses, or the commandment spoken by Jesus, to be the first and most important.

WINNIE: That means Ollie has won $3,000 to my measly $500. How can that be good news for both of us?

MC: The good news is the judges have decided to invite you both back next week for another game of *Name That Commandment!*

WINNIE: Oh goody! That means I can study with Ollie and we'll just see what happens! I could be a real winner next time!

MC: That's all the time we have for today. Thanks for joining us. We'll be giving both contestants our home game version of *Name That Commandment!* Join us next week, and don't forget: Make God's commandments the laws you live by! (*All exit.*)

• •

David Fights Goliath
by Douglas L. Wathen
SCRIPTURE REFERENCE:
1 Samuel 17:1-51

• •

TEACHER: Today we are going to hear a wonderful story about a great man from the Bible. This man won a great battle for God's people when they were at war with a terrible enemy. The story begins—

HELPER: (*Interrupting*) Oh, oh, can I help tell the story? Please! Can I? Can I? Can I? Pleeeeease?

TEACHER: Well, OK. But just how are you going to help tell the story?

HELPER: I want to be one of the people in the story. I want to be the one who wins the battle! (*Dramatically*) I want to be the jet pilot flying behind enemy lines, flying at mach eleven-teen, below enemy radar, low on fuel, bombs to the left of me, rockets to the right of me!

TEACHER: No, no, this story happened a long time ago. Way before jet planes and rockets were invented.

HELPER: You mean this happened when *you* were in high school?

TEACHER: Do you want to help tell this story or not?

HELPER: Sure I do! Who do I get to play?

TEACHER: You get to play David.

HELPER: All right! (*Singing*) I get to be David, I get to be David! (*Back to speaking*) I have just one question...who is David?

TEACHER: David is the guy who fights the battle.

HELPER: So, David is like a big huge superhero, with huge muscles, riding a big horse?

TEACHER: No, David was a teenage boy.

HELPER: A boy?

TEACHER: Yes, David's father sent him to the battle where David's brothers were fighting the Philistines.

HELPER: Why were David's brothers fighting her?

TEACHER: Her? Her who?

HELPER: Phyllis.

TEACHER: Phyllis who?

HELPER: Phyllis Steen, of course.

TEACHER: Who is Phyllis Steen?

HELPER: How should I know? This is your story.

TEACHER: Ugh! The Philistines were the armies that David's brothers were fighting. Now one of the Philistines was a giant man. He was over nine feet tall. He was big!

HELPER: He was big!

TEACHER: And he was mean!

HELPER: He was mean!

TEACHER: He was strong!

HELPER: I can smell him from here.

TEACHER: Now, every day the giant would call out to the Israelites. He challenged them to send out one warrior to fight him alone. Whoever won the fight would win the war. He would insult the Israelites and their God, but nobody would fight the giant.

HELPER: Ha, chickens!

TEACHER: Then one day someone said he would fight the giant. (*Teacher looks at the helper.*) David said he would fight the giant.

HELPER: Say what? No way! I think David said he had to go mow the cat and feed the lawn.

TEACHER: David wasn't afraid of that giant at all.

HELPER: He wasn't? But the giant was big!

TEACHER: True, but David knew he was fighting for the Lord.

He knew that with God's help he could win. So it didn't matter how big the giant was.

HELPER: I see. (*With confidence*) David was fighting for the Lord!

TEACHER: That's right!

HELPER: The giant is big!

TEACHER: Yes, he's big.

HELPER: And he's bad!

TEACHER: He was bad!

HELPER: And he stinks!

TEACHER: And he...uh...he needs a shower.

HELPER: But David was not afraid. He was fighting for the Lord!

TEACHER: David went down to the stream in the middle of the battlefield.

HELPER: David was not afraid, he was fighting for the Lord!

TEACHER: The giant laughed at David and said, "How dare you send a boy to fight me. Your God must be weak. I will crush this boy and smash him into dust, and I'll feed him to the birds."

HELPER: (*Suddenly panicked*) David was scared out of his mind! (*Calms down*) But he knew God could do anything.

TEACHER: That's right! Then do you know what David said to the giant?

HELPER: He said, "Hey Phyllis! You'd better stop insulting the Lord, or I'll feed *you* to the birds!"

TEACHER: Who is Phyllis?

HELPER: You know, the giant.

TEACHER: The giant's name was not Phyllis. His name was Goliath.

HELPER: Oh, gotcha.

TEACHER: David looked down into the stream and found his weapon. He reached down and picked up...

HELPER: A rocket launcher! He took aim and...Kabloomie!

TEACHER: No, he did not find a rocket launcher. He found a weapon that God provided for him.

HELPER: What was it?

TEACHER: A rock.

HELPER: (*Unimpressed*) A rock? You mean as in "a rock"? (*Teacher nods.*) Great, we're doomed.

TEACHER: No, no, wait just a minute. David placed the small smooth stone into a sling. He twirled it around and then let the stone fly through the air. The stone hit the giant in the head and the giant came crashing to the ground. David won the fight because he believed that God would give him the victory.

HELPER: With a rock?

TEACHER: God helps all of us each day to fight spiritual battles in our lives. Those battles would be just as hopeless for us to win as a boy fighting a giant, unless we use the weapons God gives us. David used a stone, but God gives us prayer and faith to win our battles.

HELPER: Wow, what a cool story! I guess we can all do great things if we are fighting on God's side. Even if it looks impossible.

● ●

A Night With the Lions
by Douglas L. Wathen
SCRIPTURE REFERENCE:
Daniel 6:1-24

• •

VOICE:	OK, pal, in you go! (*Daniel appears in the puppet stage as if he's been tossed in.*)
TERRY:	Well well well, you must be Daniel. We've been expecting you.
DANIEL:	You...you have?
LENNY:	Yeah! Been waiting all day.
TERRY:	My name is Terry, I'm the head lion around here. And this is Lenny, he's an assistant lion—you know, support staff.
DANIEL:	Assistant lion? I don't understand.
TERRY:	Well, you see, in the animal kingdom we have a respect for the older, wiser, and better-looking members of the species, such as myself. Being the exceptional lion, I possess the natural bravery, cunning, intelligence, and superiority to be the leader of the den.
LENNY:	Mostly, it's just 'cause he's bigger than I am.
TERRY:	Yup! So if Lenny gets out of line, Ka-bang-o! Know what I mean?
DANIEL:	So you're the leader of the den?
TERRY:	That's right, leader of the den!
DANIEL:	Well (*unsure what to say*) I...uh, love what you've done with the place.
TERRY:	It's nothing flashy, but it's home sweet home to us.
DANIEL:	I like how you made such neat little piles out of all those, um...bones.
TERRY:	That was Lenny's idea.
LENNY:	I saw that in an article in Better Dens and Gardens. But

I made it on my own.

DANIEL: So, what do you guys do here all day?

TERRY: Sleep!

LENNY: And eat criminals.

DANIEL: Eat criminals? (*Gulps.*) Is that really all you do?

LENNY: Let me see...sleep 'til noon, wake up, take a nap, wake up again, eat criminals, pace back and forth, personal quiet time, take another nap, then go to bed. Yep, that's pretty much the whole day.

DANIEL: So, uh, what does it mean to be the head lion?

TERRY: Well, as the head lion, I get to do whatever I want. If I want to stand over here, then I can. I can pace back and forth whenever I want, and when we eat, I start! Then Lenny eats what I don't want, and Lenny lets the rats have the leftovers. Only it's a bad deal for the rats, because when Lenny's done eatin' there are no leftovers! I'm not lyin'. Get it? *Ly-in'.* Ha ha. I got a million of 'em.

LENNY: Hey, Danny boy, you don't look like most criminals. You look nice and um, abundantly-proportioned.

TERRY: What he's trying to say is that you're kind of fat...you know, for a criminal.

LENNY: No, that's not what I'm trying to say. It's not nice to tell someone he's fat.

TERRY: Most of the criminals we get in here are starving beggars and thieves with no meat on their bones. You don't look like a beggar. So what are you in for?

LENNY: Didja rob a bank?

TERRY: Are you an international diamond smuggler?

DANIEL: No.

LENNY: Oh, I know! Didja forget to rewind a video?

(*Daniel and Terry stare blankly at Lenny for a few seconds.*)

LENNY: What?

TERRY: (*To Daniel*) What can I say, we don't get out much.

LENNY: So Dan, why are you in here?

DANIEL: Well, I was one of the king's advisers. It's a good job, and the king liked my advice. But all the other advisers were jealous because the king always liked my advice best. So they tricked the king into making a law that said the king was a god!

TERRY: Even we know that there is only one true living God, and that he created the whole universe. No law can change that.

DANIEL: Exactly! Well, I love the one true living God, and I pray to him many times a day. But this new law said that nobody could pray to anyone but the king! Well, I knew that I had to keep on praying to God no matter what happened to me. Even if it meant being thrown into a terrible, rotting, stinking lions' den. Uh, no offense.

TERRY: None taken.

DANIEL: I will serve the Lord, no matter what. So go ahead, do your worst. Eat me.

TERRY: Settle down, Danny, we ain't gonna eat ya.

DANIEL: You're not? But why? I'm a good meal, look at all the meat on me.

LENNY: Sorry, we can't. We got orders.

DANIEL: Orders? Orders from who?

TERRY: From the angel of the Lord.

DANIEL: Angel? What angel?

TERRY: God sent his angel just before you got here. Scared Lenny half to death.

LENNY: Stop, you're embarrassing me.

TERRY: The angel said that we shouldn't harm you in any way. And when God says don't harm you, then we're not gonna harm you. I gotta say, Dan, it took some guts to stand up for your faith. God is honoring your faith now.

LENNY: Hey look, the sun is comin' up.

KING'S VOICE: Daniel, are you there? Was your God able to save you from the lions?

DANIEL: Yes, king! I am safe; the Lord has protected me from the lions.

KING'S VOICE: Come up out of the den, Daniel.

DANIEL: Well, see ya, guys, and thanks for not eating me.

LENNY: Eh, you probably would've been a bit tough anyway.

TERRY: You just keep doin' what God says, and he'll take care of ya!

LENNY: And try to keep this "not eatin' ya" stuff to yourself. We got a reputation to maintain.

(*Daniel exits. The two lions listen to the offstage voices.*)

KING'S VOICE: Daniel, I was tricked into making that foolish law. The God you serve must be the one true God. Guards, throw these wicked advisers into the lions' den!

BOTH LIONS: (*Look at each other and gasp.*) Breakfast!

• •

A Fish Story

by Todd Liebenow

SCRIPTURE REFERENCE:
Jonah 1–4

SETTING:
A young man is fishing at the edge of a stream.

● ●

MAN:	(*Pulls line out of the water.*) Still not even a bite! Whoever said that fishing was relaxing was out of his mind. Maybe I'm using the wrong bait.
JONAH:	(*Enters.*) Good afternoon.
MAN:	Shhh, you'll scare all the fish away!
JONAH:	I'd say the fish are already scared away. Doesn't look like you've been catching much.
MAN:	That's the understatement of the year! This has to be the most frustrating thing I've ever done in my life. I can't believe I let my buddies talk me into taking up fishing. They said it would help me relax—you know, calm my nerves and all. What a joke! I don't suppose you have any pointers for me?
JONAH:	I'm afraid I'm not very good at catching fish myself. I have been caught by a fish before, but that was—
MAN:	(*Interrupting*) Wait a minute, go back just a second. Did you say you were caught by a fish?
JONAH:	Yes, but that was a long, long time ago.
MAN:	I've heard of men catching fish, but never a fish catching a man. You must really be a lousy fisherman.
JONAH:	Well, I wasn't fishing. I was floating out in the middle of the sea when a giant fish swallowed me.
MAN:	OK, then you must really be a lousy swimmer. What were you doing out in the middle of the sea?

JONAH: I had been on a ship, but I got thrown overboard. See, there was this terrible storm and I told the sailors that the storm was my fault.

MAN: How could a storm be your fault?

JONAH: Well, I was running away from God.

MAN: Don't you know you can't run away from God? I mean, he is God, after all.

JONAH: I realize that now. God told me to go to Nineveh to tell the people there about him. God said that he would destroy the city if they didn't repent. But I didn't want to go to Nineveh. I thought all the people in Nineveh were just lousy, nasty sinners who deserved whatever punishment they got.

MAN: Hey, watch it. I was born in Nineveh!

JONAH: I'm sorry. I don't feel that way anymore.

MAN: Well, good. So you mean to tell me that even though God told you to go to Nineveh, you decided not to?

JONAH: That's right, I got on a boat and headed in the other direction. That's when the storm came.

MAN: So there you were, stuck in a fish's belly. What was that like?

JONAH: It was dark, and cold, and wet. But the worst thing was the smell. If you think fish smell bad on the outside, you should take a whiff from the inside.

MAN: (*Disgusted*) Eww, stop! You'll make me sick.

JONAH: That's exactly what happened to the fish, he got sick. I spent three days and nights praying inside that fish's stomach, until finally that fish got tired of me jumping around inside and spit me out. After that I headed for Nineveh as quickly as I could.

MAN: That's using your head.

JONAH: I told the people there about God, and they repented. God decided not to destroy the city after all.

MAN: Way to go! You saved my hometown.

JONAH: I know, but I was angry at God for this. I was angry about the storm and the fish, and for God saving those people. But God spoke to me and showed me how he cares for all people, no matter who they are or what they've done. Now I wish I had done what God told me in the first place.

MAN: At least that way you wouldn't have had to smell the inside of a fish's stomach.

JONAH: That's true. Well, I'm sorry to have disturbed you. I'll let you get back to your fishing.

MAN: That's OK. Now that I know there are fish out there who can catch people, I think I'll take up bird-watching instead.

        (Both laugh and exit.)

Good News...Bad News

by Liz VonSeggen

SCRIPTURE REFERENCE:

Mark 2:1-12

• •

ROY: And now for a look at the news here in Capernaum. This is Roy.

JOY: And Joy, with the good news!

ROY: And the bad news happening every day. Well, here's the bad news: reports surfaced today of a paralyzed man who had given up hope of ever walking again. It seems he was unable to get to a doctor or hospital, and as you know, doctors are no longer making house calls.

JOY: However, the good news is that Jesus had been seen in the neighborhood, and reports have it that his healing credentials were incredible.

ROY: But the bad news is that Jesus had no plans to make a house call on the paralyzed man.

JOY: True, but the good news is this sick man had four friends who made plans to carry him to the house where Jesus was visiting.

ROY: But the bad news is that everybody in town had the same idea, and when the four men arrived with their sick friend on a cot, the crowd was so big that they could not get close to Jesus, let alone request the healer's services.

JOY: The good news is the sick man's friends promised him they would find a way for him to see Jesus face to face.

ROY: But the bad news is they carried the paralyzed man to the rooftop and tore a big hole in the roof.

JOY: How is that bad news?

ROY: It's bad news for the guy who owns that house. There's rain in the forecast.

JOY: Oh, but the good news is roofs can be repaired, and the man who couldn't walk finally had his chance to see Jesus. The four men let their friend down right in front of the crowd at Jesus' feet. Jesus said to the man, "Your sins are forgiven."

ROY: But the bad news is there were teachers of the law in the crowd who were shocked to hear Jesus say he could forgive sins. They began to mutter, "Who does he think he is? Only God can forgive sins."

JOY: But the good news is Jesus used this moment to perform a great miracle. Jesus said out loud for all to hear, "Which is easier to say, 'I forgive this man's sins,' or 'take up your bed and walk'?" The greatest good news was that the man stood up completely healed from his sickness and his sins!

ROY: I must admit the news was good for that man, but there's still a hole left in the roof!

JOY: I'd say it might become a famous museum site where they could point out the hole in their roof as a reminder of Jesus' amazing miracle.

ROY: That's a good idea. They could sell T-shirts and post-cards. Well, that's it for—

JOY: The good news!

ROY: And the bad news. After all, life is full of bad news... I just report it!

JOY: But if you discover Jesus as your personal friend, he will fill your life with the good news of his power.

ROY: So you can overcome the bad news.

He Touched Me!

by Jantzie Blue

SCRIPTURE REFERENCE:

Matthew 9:20-22

SETTING:

A hallway at school

· ·

AMANDA: Oh, I can't believe it. I was right there, center stage at the Bible Boys concert! Oh man, I will never ever ever ever forget this day!

EMILY: (*Enters.*) Hey Amanda, did I hear you went to the Bible Boys concert? Wow, that must have been really cool. I just love their songs.

AMANDA: Oh Emily, it was sooooo incredible! And you know what? The guitarist, Matthew James, touched me! (*Lets out a teenage shriek.*) He shook my hand after the show! Oh, I am never going to wash this hand again. (*Raises arm to show that her hand is wrapped in a plastic bag.*)

EMILY: Ummm...Amanda, why is there a plastic bag on your hand?

AMANDA: Because, silly, it has Matthew James' fingerprints, smells, and other stuff all over it. I am never gonna wash this hand, ever!

EMILY: Don't you think that is just a little silly? I mean, forever is a very long time. You will never be able to pet your kitty and feel how soft and cuddly it is. Or what about when you pick flowers for your mom? How are you going to hold them? Or how are you going to write in your journal? In fact, how are you going to do anything with a plastic bag over your hand? Huh?

AMANDA: (*Pauses.*) I'll use my toes. They are just down there doing nothing anyway.

EMILY: (*Sighs.*) Amanda, you just don't get it.

AMANDA: Yes I do. Why, I just learned in Sunday school about how Jesus was just walking through a crowd of people, and this woman reached out and just touched his robe and was healed. Just by touching his robe!

EMILY: But Amanda, the Bible Boys are not Jesus! Oh sure, they are gorgeous and dreamy, and their singing...what a gift. (*Sighs, then comes back to reality.*) But they're not healers, they're just performers. Don't you remember in Mark 5:25, Jesus was going to see a little girl who was sick and dying, and there were crowds of people around the streets? A woman was there who was very ill, and she thought if she just touched his robe she would be healed. So she did. Just by touching Jesus' robe, she felt in her body that she was freed from her suffering. At once, Jesus realized power had left him. He turned around in the crowd and asked, "Who touched my clothes?" I bet that Matthew James never even saw you at the concert, let alone knew that you touched him.

AMANDA: But he touched me!

EMILY: Uggggggghh!

AMANDA: OK, I know that Matthew James or any of the others from the Bible Boys are not Jesus, and wearing this plastic bag on my hand has gotten a few stares...but c'mon...Matthew James! Oh, he is sooooo dreamy! And besides, how many other girls around here can say that he touched them, huh?

(*Three other girls pass by, doing the teenage shriek, wearing plastic bags on their hands, and all saying, "Matthew James touched me!" or variations. They exit.*)

EMILY: Apparently a lot.

AMANDA: (*Surprised, then sad*) I feel so silly.

EMILY: Oh Amanda, don't feel silly. Just remember that Jesus was a wonderful healer, and that the power of his healing was much deeper than just his clothing.

AMANDA: And that plastic bags are for sandwiches, not hands.

(*Both girls laugh as they exit together.*)

• •

A Picnic for Five Thousand

by Randy Benefield

SCRIPTURE REFERENCES:

Matthew 14:13-21; John 6:1-13

SETTING:

Kitchen of a small house

• •

BOY: (*Running in*) Mama, can we go to the park today? Please!

MAMA: I don't know, son; better go ask your father.

BOY: OK! (*Runs across stage to his father's work area.*) Papa, Papa! Can we go to the park today? Can we? Pleeeease, can we?

PAPA: Oh, I don't know, son. I've got a lot to do around here. You'd better go ask your mother.

BOY: Okey-dokey! (*Running back across to the kitchen*) Mama...Mama, Papa said it's OK with him, if it's OK with you.

MAMA: Really? Well, I guess if your father said it's all right, then it's OK with me! This could be kind of fun.

BOY: Great! I'll go tell Papa. (*Running back to other side of stage, somewhat out of breath*) Mama said it's OK with her, Papa!

PAPA: (*Surprised*) She did? Oh, that's good...I guess? Well then, I suppose we should pack a few things: beach chairs, blanket, sunscreen—

BOY: (*Interrupting*) Can we bring a picnic lunch? Please, can we?

PAPA: Maybe. Go ask your mother if we have any of that fish left.

BOY: (*Running back to Mama*) Mama, Papa says we should take some of those fish he caught. Just in case we get hungry.

MAMA: I don't know if I have anything to go with them, son. I haven't had a chance to go to the market. (*Looking around*) I only have these two fish left, and let's see...two, three, four, it looks like only four small loaves of bread.

BOY: I've got a loaf in my room. I was going to have it for a snack, but now that we're going to the park, we can take it along. That will give us a total of five loaves.

MAMA: And only two fishes!

BOY: It'll be enough, Mama. I'll go pack my stuff. Be back in a minute. (*Exits.*)

MAMA: (*To herself*) I just love picnics, but I hate rushing to get ready. (*Looking*) Now, where did I put that picnic basket? Oh, here it is. OK, two fish and five pieces of bread. I've got a small jug of water. I think we're set!

PAPA: (*Crossing over to Mama*) I'm all finished in the workshop. You about ready in here?

MAMA: Just about. I'm taking the bread and fish. Hope we have some left over for tomorrow!

BOY: (*Entering*) I'm all packed. Should I take my fishing pole?

PAPA: Sure! Bring it along. Just don't ask me to carry it!

(*All exit and then re-enter in the park.*)

PAPA: Wow! Would you look at all these people? Looks like some kind of convention or something.

MAMA: I guess everyone else had the same idea we did. I just hate it when the park is crowded.

BOY: Maybe it's a classic chariot show. I'll go check it out. Be back in a few. (He *runs ahead across stage as the parents exit—and bumps into Andrew.*)

ANDREW: Slow down, my friend! Where are you going in such a rush?

BOY: Sorry, mister. I was just trying to see what's going on.

ANDREW: You can call me Andrew, and I can tell you what's happening. Jesus of Nazareth is here. What's in your basket there, son?

BOY: Just some food for me and my parents. Why?

ANDREW: These people have been following Jesus for a long time. They are tired and hungry, and he would like to feed them.

BOY: Well, you can have our lunch, if you want.

ANDREW: That's very nice of you. What do you have?

BOY: Just five loaves of bread and two fishes that my dad caught.

ANDREW: I hardly think it would feed the likes of this crowd.

BOY: Why, don't they like fish?

ANDREW: There are thousands of people here. What you have wouldn't even feed my brother, Peter. He has a big appetite sometimes.

BOY: Well, I've heard about this man called Jesus. He's supposed to be pretty amazing. Why don't you ask him and see what he thinks?

ANDREW: Very well! You wait here and I'll go ask him. (*Exits.*)

BOY: (*To himself as he paces*) Well, it was worth a try. I never met anyone famous before. Maybe I could get Jesus' autograph. It could be worth something someday.

ANDREW: (*Returning*) Jesus says he likes your style, son. Says you got faith. He likes that. He wants to meet you. Come with me, and bring those loaves and fishes. I have a feeling something amazing is about to happen.

(*Both exit as parents enter.*)

MAMA: I think he went this way, dear.

PAPA: I don't see him. We'd better just wait here. He'll be back in a few minutes.

MAMA: I hope so.

PAPA: Me too. He's got all the food with him!

  (*Both exit.*)

● ●

Hide and Seek

by Liz VonSeggen

SCRIPTURE REFERENCE:

Luke 15:3-7

SHEEP #99: (*Hiding his eyes*) Ninety-seven...ninety-eight...ninety-nine...one hundred. Who's not ready, holler I? (*Looks up and begins to look around the stage for other sheep.*)

SHEEP #100: (*From hiding place*) Ba-a-a-a. He'll never find me.

SHEEP #99: Where, oh where could all the sheep be hiding? Not behind the big bushes. (*Going below stage*) Not down here in the ditch. I don't see a single lamb's hoofprint to tell me where they headed. I thought this would be easy. Why, this field is as flat as Kansas. No trees, no barns, not even a haystack to hide inside. Baa-a—aa-a-a!

SHEEP #100: (*Calling from behind the stage*) Hey, Lamb Chops. Look ba-a-a-ack here!

SHEEP #99: (*Looking around the stage*) Who said tha-a-at? (*Turns to audience.*) Did you see a big fa-a-a-at ram or a little la-a-a-amb?

SHEPHERD: (*Enters.*) There you are, Number 99. I've just counted ninety-eight sheep in for the night and now you're ninety-nine. Where's Sheep 100?

SHEEP #99: Tha-a-a-at's a good question. We're playing Hide-and-Seek, and I thought it would be real easy to find all the sheep out here in this fla-a-a-at land. But I can't seem to find Number 100. He sure did find a good hiding place.

SHEPHERD: Why don't I help you look for him? It's getting dark, and I need to be sure all one hundred sheep are in the fold before the stars come out tonight. It's not too safe out here with the wolves that roam these fields after dark.

SHEEP #99: Aw, don't worry about Sheep 100. He can take care of himself. Why, he's sneaky enough to fleece the fur right off any big bad wolf in the territory.

SHEPHERD: I know Sheep 100. He is clever, but I don't want to take any chances with my sheep. You see, little one, every lamb is important to me, and I can't sleep until I've counted all one hundred sheep safe in the sheep-fold with me. Then and only then can I lie down and rest.

SHEEP #99: I guess that's the difference between you and me, Mr. Shepherd. I'm going to head into the fold right now and start counting sheep in my sleep. You, on the other hand, can do whatever you decide about finding that lost sheep who doesn't want to be found! (*Exits.*)

SHEPHERD: Calling all sheep...come out, come out wherever you are. You win. Game's over!

WOLF: Aooooo! (*Comes sneaking in.*) Here I am, Detective Wolfgang at your service, sir, specializing in finding lost sheep. (*Laughs in a sinister way.*)

SHEPHERD: You don't say. I won't be needing your services, because you are precisely the reason I am here to find my own lost sheep. I have come to help my lost sheep find his way.

WOLF: Oh, but you don't understand me, I'm sure. I, too, have come to help him find his way...(*to audience*) into my stomach!

(*Sheep 100 runs out toward the shepherd, but the wolf captures the sheep in his mouth.*)

SHEPHERD: You have come to kill and destroy. I will give my life for my sheep. Stand back, Mr. Wolf. (*He pulls out a Bible and holds it up at the head of the wolf.*)

WOLF: Ahhhhhhh! (*Drops sheep.*) How was I to know you had a sword? I'm outta here. But I'll be back when you're not around! (*Yelps as he limps out.*)

SHEPHERD: I will never leave or forsake this sheep. Get out of my sight, wolf!

WOLF: Rats! Those rotten shepherds are always getting in the way!

SHEEP #100: Baa-a-a-ad wolf! Go-o-o-od Shepherd! Could we go back to the fold now?

SHEPHERD: Just follow me, Sheep 100!

(They exit.)

A P P E N D I X

Puppet Ministry Resources

The following resources represent some of the best available material on puppets and puppet ministry. You'll find many of the books and other resources at your local Christian bookstore, puppet ministry suppliers, or you can order them from the publishers.

Books

Easy-to-Make Puppets by Fran Rottman. A classroom teacher resource for ministry to young children using sack, sock, paper bag, glove, rod, and various other very simple puppets. Published by Gospel Light, 2300 Knoll Dr., Ventura, CA 93003.

Instant Puppet Skits: 20 Stories From People Who Met Jesus by Mikal Keefer and John Cutshall. A great book for beginning puppet ministry teams. Twenty skits based on encounters with Jesus. Includes two CDs that offer complete dialogue and sound effects. Provides discussion questions for follow-up and further learning with each skit. Published by Group Publishing, P.O. Box 481, Loveland, CO 80539.

Puppet Director's Notebook by Dale VonSeggen and Jim Scott. Aimed at adults desiring to organize older children and teens into ongoing team ministry. Contains helpful advice, record-keeping forms, and an excellent merit system for puppeteers. Published by One Way Street, Inc., P.O. Box 5077, Englewood, CO 80155.

Worlds of Shadow by David Wisniewski and Donna Wisniewski. Focuses on the many aspects of using shadow puppetry. Includes step-by-step instructions, scenes, patterns, and drawings. Published by Libraries Unlimited (Teacher Ideas Press), 88 Post Road West, Westport, CT 06881.

Other Materials

Puppet Props and Scenery with Dave Privett. This training video provides step-by-step instructions for making simple signs and props to enhance your puppet performances. Dave demonstrates prop-building techniques and gives many source tips for prop making in general. Published by Playsoup Productions, P.O. Box 4351, Englewood, CO 80155.

Reaching and Teaching with Puppets featuring Dale and Liz VonSeggen. This two-hour training video covers all aspects of training puppeteers and developing a puppet ministry. It includes several performance segments and is available from One Way Street, Inc., P.O. Box 5077, Englewood, CO 80155.

Target Trax, Righteous Pop Music, and *Puppets in Action.* These three compact disc series contain songs and skits produced for puppet ministry use. They are available from One Way Street, Inc., P.O. Box 5077, Englewood, CO 80155

Puppetry Suppliers

Maher Ventriloquist Studios
P.O. Box 420
Littleton, CO 80160
www.maherstudios.com

Mastercraft Puppets
P.O. Box 2002
Branson, MO 65615
www.mastercraftpuppets.com

One Way Street, Inc.
P.O. Box 5077
Englewood, CO 80155
www.onewaystreet.com

Puppet Productions
P.O. Box 1066
DeSoto, TX 75123
www.puppetproductions.com

Son Shine Puppet Company
P.O. Box 6203
Rockford, IL 61125
www.sonshinepuppetco.com

Train Depot
3244 Commerce Center Place
Louisville, KY 40211
www.traindepot.org

Organizations and Conferences

International Festival of Christian
Puppetry and Ventriloquism
P.O. Box 5077
Englewood, CO 80155
www.onewaystreet.com

Fellowship of Christian Magicians
7739 Everest Court North
Maple Grove, MN 55311
www.fcm.org

Fellowship of Christian Puppeteers
107 Moore Allen St.
Dudley, NC 28333
www.fcpfellowship.org

Puppeteers of America
P.O. Box 29417
Parma, OH 44129
www.puppeteers.org

Group Publishing, Inc.
Attention: Product Development
P.O. Box 481
Loveland, CO 80539
Fax: (970) 679-4370

Evaluation for
Puppet Ministry Made Easy

Please help Group Publishing, Inc. continue to provide innovative and useful resources for ministry. Please take a moment to fill out this evaluation and mail or fax it to us. Thanks!

● ● ●

1. As a whole, this book has been (circle one)
not very helpful   very helpful

| 1 | 2 | 3 | 4 | 5 | 6 | 7 | 8 | 9 | 10 |

2. The best things about this book:

3. Ways this book could be improved:

4. Things I will change because of this book:

5. Other books I'd like to see Group publish in the future:

Name _____

Church Name _____

Denomination _____ Church Size _____

Church Address_____

City _____ State _____ ZIP _____

Church Phone _____

E-mail _____